Decorative Art

RIGHT PAGE / RECHTE SEITE / PAGE DE DROITE:
Marcel Breuer, *Model No. B33* Chair for Gebrüder Thonet, 1927–1928

Editorial note:
The dates shown in the footers on the reprinted pages relate only to the year of publication and not to the year of design for the artifacts included.

Anmerkung der Herausgeber:
Die Jahreszahlen in den Kolumnentiteln geben das Erscheinungsjahr der Zeitschrift und nicht das Entstehungsjahr der Objekte an.

Note éditoriale:
Les dates indiquées en bas des pages renvoient à celles de publication et non à celles de création des objets concernés.

Design: UNA (London) designers
Production: Martina Ciborowius, Cologne
Editorial coordination: Susanne Husemann, Cologne
© for the introduction: Charlotte and Peter Fiell, London
German translation by Uta Hoffmann, Cologne
French translation by Philippe Safavi, Paris

Printed in Italy
ISBN 3–8228–6051–4

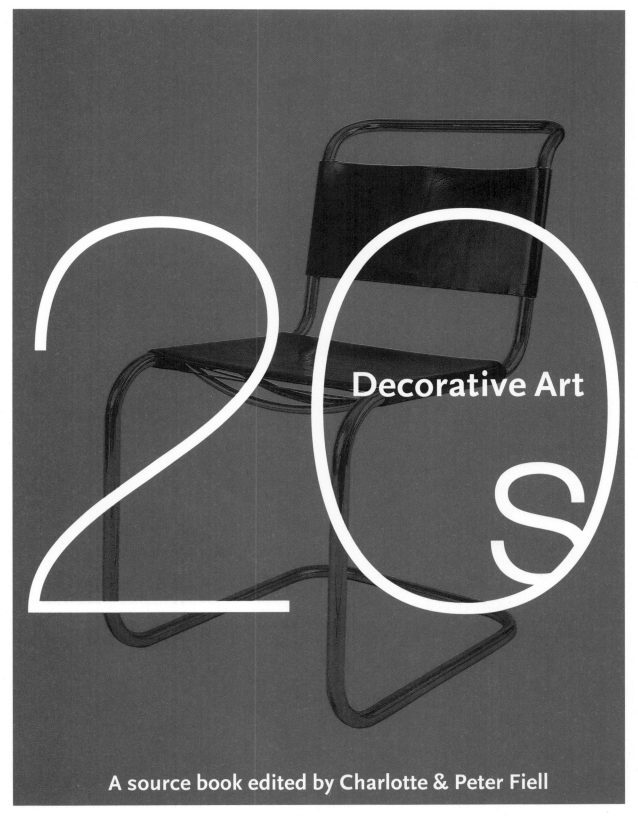

20s

Decorative Art

A source book edited by Charlotte & Peter Fiell

TASCHEN

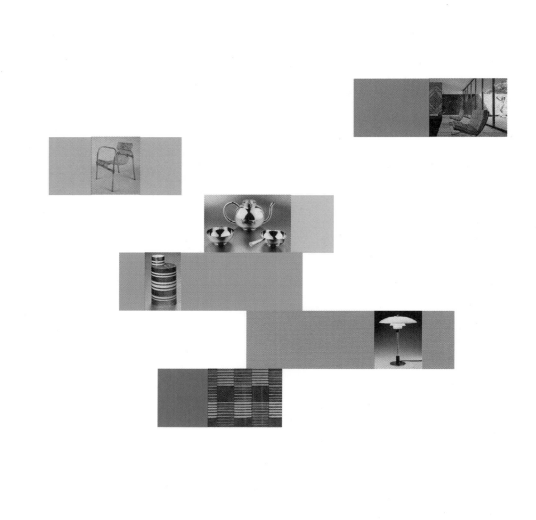

CONTENTS
INHALT
SOMMAIRE

PREFACE

PAGE / SEITE 4:
Walter Gropius, Staircase in the Feininger-Haus, Meistersiedlung Dessau, 1926
PAGE / SEITE 5:
Wilhelm Wagenfeld, *MT9/ME1* table lamp for the Bauhaus Dessau, 1923–1924
LEFT PAGE / LINKE SEITE / PAGE DE GAUCHE:
Poul Henningsen, *PH* table lamp for Louis Poulsen, c. 1927
BOTTOM / UNTEN / EN BAS:
Lena Bergner, Design for a textile, 1928

The "Decorative Art" Yearbooks

The Studio Magazine was founded in Britain in 1893 and featured both the fine and the decorative arts. It initially promoted the work of progressive designers such as Charles Rennie Mackintosh and Charles Voysey to a wide audience both at home and abroad, and was especially influential in Continental Europe. Later, in 1906, *The Studio* began publishing the *Decorative Art* yearbook to "meet the needs of that ever-increasing section of the public who take interest in the application of art to the decoration and general equipment of their homes". This annual survey, which became increasingly international in its outlook, was dedicated to the latest currents in architecture, interiors, furniture, lighting, glassware, textiles, metalware and ceramics. From its outset, *Decorative Art* advanced the "New Art" that had been pioneered by William Morris and his followers, and attempted to exclude designs which showed any "excess in ornamentation and extreme eccentricities of form".

In the 1920s, *Decorative Art* began promoting Modernism and was in later years a prominent champion of "Good Design". Published from the 1950s onwards by Studio Vista, the yearbooks continued to provide a remarkable overview of each decade, featuring avant-garde and often experimental designs alongside more mainstream products. Increasing prominence was also lent to architecture and interior design, and in the mid-1960s the title of the series was changed to *Decorative Art in Modern Interiors* to reflect this shift in emphasis. Eventually, in 1980, Studio Vista ceased publication of these unique annuals, and over the succeeding years volumes from the series became highly prized by collectors and dealers as excellent period reference sources.

The fascinating history of design traced by *Decorative Art* can now be accessed once again in this new series, reprinted in a somewhat revised form from the original yearbooks. In line with the layout of *Decorative Art*, the various disciplines are grouped separately, whereby great care has been taken to select the best and most interesting pages while ensuring that the corresponding dates have been given due prominence for ease of reference. It is important to remember that the dates shown in the footers on the reprinted pages relate only to the year of publication and not to the year of design for the artifacts included. Finally, it is hoped that these volumes of highlights from *Decorative Art* will at long last bring the yearbooks to a wider audience, who will find in them well-known favourites as well as fascinating and previously unknown designs.

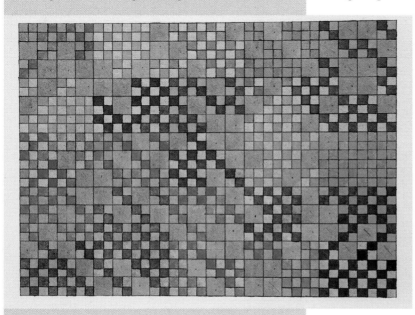

VORWORT

Die »Decorative Art«-Jahrbücher

Die Zeitschrift *The Studio Magazine* wurde 1893 in England gegründet und war sowohl der Kunst als auch dem Kunsthandwerk gewidmet. In den Anfängen stellte sie einer breiten Öffentlichkeit in England und in Übersee die Arbeiten progressiver Designer wie Charles Rennie Mackintosh und Charles Voysey vor. Ihr Einfluss war groß und nahm auch auf dem europäischen Festland zu. 1906 begann *The Studio* zusätzlich mit der Herausgabe des *Decorative Art Yearbook*, um »den Bedürfnissen einer ständig wachsenden Öffentlichkeit gerecht zu werden, die sich zunehmend dafür interessierte, Kunst in die Dekoration und Ausstattung ihrer Wohnungen einzubeziehen.« Diese jährlichen Überblicke unterrichteten über die neuesten internationalen Tendenzen in der Architektur und Innenraumgestaltung, bei Möbeln, Lampen, Glas und Keramik, Metall und Textilien. Von Anfang an förderte *Decorative Art* die von William Morris und seinen Anhängern entwickelte »Neue Kunst« und versuchte, Entwürfe auszuschließen, die »in Mustern und Formen zu überladen und exzentrisch waren.«

In den zwanziger Jahren hatte sich *Decorative Art* für modernistische Strömungen eingesetzt und wurde in der Folgezeit zu einer prominenten Befürworterin des »guten Designs«. Die seit 1950 vom englischen Verlag Studio Vista veröffentlichten Jahrbücher stellten für jedes Jahrzehnt ausgezeichnete Überblicke der vorherrschenden avantgardistischen und experimentellen Trends im Design einerseits und des bereits in der breiteren Öffentlichkeit etablierten Alltagsdesigns andererseits zusammen. Als Architektur und Interior Design Mitte der sechziger Jahre ständig an Bedeutung gewannen, wurde die Serie in *Decorative Art in Modern Interiors* umbenannt, um diesem Bedeutungswandel gerecht zu werden. Im Jahre 1981 stellte Studio Vista die Veröffentlichung dieser einzigartigen Jahrbücher ein. Sie wurden in den folgenden Jahren als wertvolle Sammelobjekte und hervorragende Nachschlagewerke, besonders auch für die Zuschreibung von Designern und Herstellern, hochgeschätzt.

Die faszinierende Geschichte des Designs, die *Decorative Art* dokumentierte, erscheint jetzt als leicht veränderter Nachdruck der originalen Jahrbücher. Dem ursprünglichen Layout von *Decorative Art* folgend, werden die einzelnen Disziplinen getrennt vorgestellt. Mit großer Sorgfalt wurden die besten und interessantesten Seiten ausgewählt. Um die zeitliche Einordung zu ermöglichen, ist das Veröffentlichungsjahr der gezeigten Objekte im Kolumnentitel angegeben. Dabei handelt es sich aber nicht um das Entstehungsjahr. Mit diesen Bänden soll einer breiten Leserschaft der Zugang zu den *Decorative Art*-Jahrbüchern und seinen international berühmt gewordenen, aber auch den weniger bekannten und dennoch faszinierenden Entwürfen ermöglicht werden.

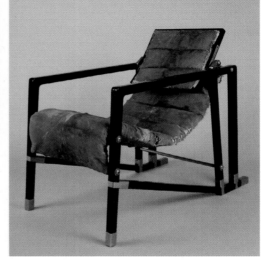

PRÉFACE

BOTTOM / UNTEN / EN BAS:
Paul Frankl, *Skyscraper* bookcase, c. 1928

Les annuaires « Decorative Art »

Fondé en 1893 en Grande-Bretagne, *The Studio Magazine* traitait à la fois des beaux-arts et des arts décoratifs. Sa vocation première était de promouvoir le travail de créateurs qui innovaient, tels que Charles Rennie Mackintosh ou Charles Voysey, auprès d'un vaste public d'amateurs tant en Grande-Bretagne qu'à l'étranger, notamment en Europe où son influence était particulièrement forte. En 1906, *The Studio* lança *The Decorative Art Yearbook*, un annuaire destiné à répondre à « la demande de cette part toujours croissante du public qui s'intéresse à l'application de l'art à la décoration et à l'aménagement général de la maison ». Ce rapport annuel, qui prit une ampleur de plus en plus internationale, était consacré aux dernières tendances en matière d'architecture, de décoration d'intérieur, de mobilier, de luminaires, de verrerie, de textiles, d'orfèvrerie et de céramique. D'emblée, *Decorative Art* mit en avant « l'Art nouveau » dont William Morris et ses disciples avaient posé les jalons, et tenta d'exclure tout style marqué par « une ornementation surchargée et des formes d'une excentricité excessive ».

Dès les années 20, *Decorative Art* commença à promouvoir le modernisme, avant de se faire le chantre du « bon design ». Publiés à partir des années 50 par Studio Vista, les annuaires continuèrent à présenter un remarquable panorama de chaque décennie, faisant se côtoyer les créations avant-gardistes et souvent expérimentales et les produits plus « grand public ». Ses pages accordèrent également une part de plus en plus grande à l'architecture et à la décoration d'intérieur. Ce changement de politique éditoriale se refléta dans le titre adopté vers le milieu des années 60 : *Decorative Art in Modern Interiors*. En 1980, Studio Vista arrêta la parution de ces volumes uniques en leur genre qui, au fil des années, devinrent très recherchés par les collectionneurs et les marchands car ils constituaient d'excellents ouvrages de référence pour les objets d'époque.

Grâce à cette réédition sous une forme légèrement modifiée, la fascinante histoire du design retracée par *Decorative Art* est de nouveau disponible. Conformément à la maquette originale des annuaires, les différentes disciplines sont présentées séparément, classées par date afin de faciliter les recherches. On souligne au passage que les dates indiquées en bas des pages rééditées renvoient à celles de publication et non à celles de création des objets concernés. Enfin, on ne peut qu'espérer que ces volumes présentent les plus belles pages de *Decorative Art* feront connaître ces annuaires à un plus vaste public, qui y retrouvera des pièces de design devenues célèbres et en découvrira d'autres inconnues auparavant et tout aussi fascinantes.

INTRODUCTION
THE 1920s

Reconstruction, Industrialisation and Standardisation

The 1920s were optimistic years in which people looked to the future and put their trust and hopes in technological progress. While the devastation of the First World War had changed society irrevocably, it also had the effect of accelerating the transition from the Edwardian era to the Modern Age. At the start of the decade motorcars were still sharing roadways with horse-drawn vehicles, and although there was electric street lighting, the majority of homes used gas or oil lamps. While most households possessed a gramophone, telephones and wireless radios were still relatively uncommon, and news and public information was disseminated largely through newsreel screenings at cinemas, which were of course also very popular for the black and white films they showed. Within the home, interiors tended to be cluttered with heavy furniture and decorative objects, while heating was provided by either labour-intensive wood-burning stoves or coal fires. As the 1920s advanced, however, huge technological advances were achieved; by the end of the decade, significantly more people had access to domestic electricity, cars and wirelesses, while a privileged minority even had the luxury of refrigerators.

It was nevertheless a decade of much hardship. The early 1920s were marked by an acute housing shortage and a lack of new furniture. Germany was utterly impoverished by the reparations imposed on it by the Armistice and the Treaty of Versailles, and between 1922 and 1923 found itself in the grip of hyperinflation. This culminated in the issuing of banknotes in denominations of up to 1 million Reichsmarks, rendering the savings of the middle-classes all but worthless. Against this generally bleak backdrop, Berlin paradoxically became the most permissive and titillating city in Europe. Its notorious cabarets revelled in a heady decadence that led the city to become known as the "Modern Babylon".

Dramatic price increases also hit the people of Britain in the early 1920s, as a consequence of shortages of both materials and manpower. The government also increased taxation to help pay for the war. The re-distribution of money had a considerable impact upon the lifestyles of each stratum of society. Just as the economic situation forced commercial enterprises to downsize, so the upper middle classes, now less prosperous because of higher taxes, began to recognise the need for smaller and more efficiently planned

RIGHT PAGE / RECHTE SEITE / PAGE DE DROITE:
Hilda Jesser, Ceramic vase for Wiener Werkstätte, c. 1928
BOTTOM / UNTEN / EN BAS:
Josef Hoffmann, Silver fruit-cup for the Wiener Werkstätte, 1924–1925

homes. During this period, the scarcity of domestic staff led to a huge demand for labour-saving devices, such as washing machines and carpet cleaners, which went a long way towards compensating for the lack of help around the home.

With less disposable income, the upper middle classes could no longer afford to patronise the decorative arts to the extent that they had previously done. As a result, many designers began producing more affordable, democratic designs that were intended to have a universal appeal. In the sphere of architecture, it was patently clear that the huge post-war requirement for affordable housing and furniture could only be met if architects and designers embraced industrialisation and standardisation. But while the public was prepared to accept new, forward-looking appliances, it nevertheless remained, for the most part, ultra-conservative in its taste, and was less willing to embrace the pared-down aesthetic of Modernism when applied to architecture and domestic furnishings. An emerging Modern style could nevertheless be detected in the design of suburban homes, which were often influenced by the earlier work of such architects as Charles Voysey. Homes such as these had plain unadorned surfaces and were frequently built as bungalows to save on cost. During the early 1920s, however, national and regional characteristics in design continued to persist: British design was simple, austere, well-made and inspired by vernacularism; French design was high-quality, luxurious and opulent; German and Austrian design was classical, heavy and geometric. It was not until around 1927 that the International Style emerged and the universal language of Functionalism became dominant within the avant-garde.

Exuberance and Luxury

The Modern Movement buildings illustrated in the *Decorative Art* yearbooks of the late 1920s were very rare examples; most architectural patrons, especially in Britain and America, continued to prefer either the Arts & Crafts style or the Art Deco style. The term Art Deco was coined from the title of an exhibition held in Paris in 1925 – the *Exposition Internationale des Arts Décoratifs et Industriels Modernes* – and described a glamorous style that was characterised by the use of exotic materials, such as mother-of-pearl and shagreen, as well as bold geometric forms. Unlike the earlier Art Nouveau movement, which had been inspired by vernacularism and natural organic forms, Art Deco drew upon an eclectic range of sources which included Egyptian and African art, Futurism, Cubism, Neo-Classicism and even Modernism. In comparison to the post-war Art Deco opalescent glassware of Réne Lalique, which possessed a sense of mass and relied on strong geometric forms, the earlier pre-war Art Nouveau cameo glassware of Émile Gallé, with its floral motifs and soft, undulating organic forms, was delicately feminine.

In the mid-1920s, French design came very much to the fore with the avant-garde generally being concentrated in Paris. Receiving patronage from a wealthy clientele including the French couturiers Paul Poiret and Jacques Douce, the greatest exponents of the sumptuous Art Deco style, such as Jacques-Émile Ruhlmann and Sue et Mare, revived their country's *décorateur* tradition with their superlative craftsmanship and use of luxury materials. With its strong associations with *haute couture*, French Art Deco was both flamboyant and luxurious and became extremely influential. It continued to inspire both English and American designers well into the 1930s, although the high-quality execution and sheer brio of the earlier French designs was rarely matched. Other designers active in the late 1920s, such as Eileen Gray and Edgar Brandt, worked in a transitional style that bridged Art Deco and Modernism – their bold designs borrowed from the aesthetic of Modernism yet remained fundamentally decorative.

LEFT PAGE / LINKE SEITE / PAGE DE GAUCHE:
Walter Gropius, Bauhaus building in Dessau, 1925–1926
BOTTOM / UNTEN / EN BAS:
Marcel Breuer, *Model No. B32* & *Model No. B64* chairs for Gebrüder Thonet, 1928

The majority of interiors during the 1920s were relatively ornamental, with fashionable patchwork cushions and appliqués textiles in bright colours bringing much-needed colour. Textiles manufactured by the Wiener Werkstätte in Vienna and Foxtons in London were also brightly coloured and often had abstracted floral patterning. Bold colour combinations inspired by contemporary art, such as ultramarine and black or black and white, became increasingly fashionable, as did eccentric geometric forms that were frequently bizarre in appearance. Although design reformers despaired of the tendency within the Art Deco style to pursue originality for originality's sake, the style that had little to do with industrial production did influence mainstream taste through its association with glamour.

Unlike Europe, America prospered considerably after the First World War. By the 1920s it had the largest gold reserves in the world and its citizens were enjoying unprecedented freedom and wealth. The notion of the "American Dream" was tirelessly pursued and was best symbolised by the building of massive skyscrapers, particularly in New York and Chicago, which were the technical marvels of their day. The spirit of the Jazz Age perhaps found its most sublime expression in the soaring Chrysler Building (1928–1930) in New York designed by William van Alen. This exuberant Art Deco structure became a totem of booming corporate America – the antithesis of what the European avant-garde stood for at this time. The Moderne style – a form of Art Deco stylistically inspired by the Modern Movement – also flourished in the United States during the late 1920s and early 1930s. As with Art Deco,

Hollywood film sets helped popularise this modernistic style, which was most often distinguished by the use of glass and gleaming chromium surfaces.

Form Follows Function

Between 1914 and 1920 building costs in Britain rose around 400%. The consequent search for cheaper and more efficient buildings led to the introduction of concrete, which was suited to arched construction – a more economical means of carrying loads than the beams traditionally employed in brick houses. Arched-construction buildings were not only structurally stronger, they also used 50–100% less materials. Concrete also had the added advantage of being fireproof, weatherproof and virtually maintenance-free. Because concrete was not subject to the same physical limitations as timber, stone or brick, it also offered greater expressive potential to the architect. Although in 1920 only a few buildings had been realized in this new and exciting material, by the end of the decade it had become the material of choice among architects associated with the Modern Movement.

Design reform was considered a social necessity by adherents of the Modern Movement, and organisations such as the Deutscher Werkbund as well as publications like the *Decorative Art* yearbooks unflaggingly promoted the Functionalist cause. The Bauhaus Exhibition of 1923 proved perhaps the most significant turning-point in the history of Modern design, as it brought widespread international attention to the new movement for the first time. Modern Movement designers in Germany, Holland, France and Britain, including Walter Gropius, Marcel Breuer, Gerrit Rietveld, J.J.P. Oud, Le Corbusier, Charlotte Perriand and Ambrose Heal, all pioneered a new approach to architecture and design that rigorously opposed the decorative excesses of the contemporaneous Art Deco style. Their designs were characterised by a stark utilitarian simplicity that was born out of American architect Louis H. Sullivan's earlier dictum that "form follows function". Houses became "machines for living" while furniture was conceived as "equipment for living". Remaining truthful to the new materials (concrete, plate glass, tubular metal) and the innovative methods of production now available, Modern Movement designers produced buildings and objects that possessed a formal vocabulary based on classical geometry (the square, cube, circle, cylinder, cone and triangle), which also looked to the future. Ceramics, for example, now typically had simple, undecorated forms that strongly contrasted with the showiness of previous Victorian lithographic transfer printing.

Protagonists of Modernism desired utility and beauty in objects without the futility of ornament, and their furniture – such as the ubiquitous tubular metal side chair – was intended to be as much in tune with 20th-century living patterns as it was with modern manufacturing methods. Mechanisation was the new reality as Shirley Wainwright acknowledged when writing in *Decorative Art* in 1923: "So far as the general needs of the public are concerned, machinery entirely dominates production and cannot be dispensed with. The most valuable contributions, therefore, to the welfare of industrial art in the future must be rooted in the frank recognition of such facts. Further developments in applied art will inevitably be democratic in their tendencies." Modernists believed that they could offer relief from the plethora of low-quality and often kitsch products through their industrially produced, high-integrity democratic designs. It was even recommended in the yearbooks that one small room should be set aside in every house as a "Chamber of Horrors" to serve as a repository for inappropriate objects with sentimental attachment. Art for Art's Sake was now replaced with an ethos based on Art for Society's Sake. Through the strength of advertising, the general public became more accepting of Modern design and increasingly desired the qualities of "fitness, utility and beauty" in the objects with which they surrounded themselves. By the mid-1920s it was realised, especially in France and Germany, that Good Design meant good business, and numerous established manufacturers began to produce truly Modern designs. Even in Britain and America, Modern design was seen as a necessary and logical development – not just by an up-and-coming generation of architects and designers, but by enthusiasts of all ages.

In Stuttgart, in 1927, the Deutscher Werkbund staged a unique exhibition entitled *Die Wohnung* (The Dwelling), organised by Ludwig Mies van der Rohe. The focus of the exhibition was a housing estate project, the Weißenhofsiedlung, for which the most progressive architects throughout Europe were invited to design buildings. The houses and

their interiors, furnished with designs by Mart Stam, Marcel Breuer and Le Corbusier, to name but a few, were widely publicised and included in the 1929 issue of *Decorative Art*. The exhibition led to a greater acceptance of Modernism, which by the following decade had became a truly international style. Insofar as they conceived buildings and objects in a scientific or mathematical way rather than from an artistic or emotional standpoint, designers associated with the Modern Movement, such as Le Corbusier and Walter Gropius, nevertheless reduced architecture and design to something of a formula-driven practice. The buildings they created with their lightweight steel frames, reinforced concrete and plate glass walls had a sterile rather than homely character and provided functionality without too many creature comforts. The Modernists' house of the future, with its scientifically equipped kitchens and built-in cupboards, required little furniture and was typified by a sense of symmetry, cleanliness and light – the humble home, it seemed, had at long last been transfigured into a truly industrialised product.

EINLEITUNG
DIE 20er JAHRE

Wiederaufbau, Industrialisierung und Standardisierung

Die 20er Jahre waren eine Zeit des Aufbruchs, in der die Menschen mit großem Optimismus in die Zukunft blickten und ihre Hoffnungen vertrauensvoll auf den technischen Fortschritt setzten. Die Verwüstungen des Ersten Weltkriegs hatten gesellschaftliche Veränderungen eingeleitet, die nicht mehr rückgängig zu machen waren, und so den Übergang von der »Edwardian« Ära zur Moderne beschleunigt. Zu Beginn des Jahrzehnts teilten Autos die Straße noch mit Pferdegespannen. Und obwohl es bereits elektrische Straßenbeleuchtungen gab, brannten in den meisten Haushalten immer noch Gas- oder Öllampen. Viele Haushalte besaßen zwar schon ein Grammophon, aber Telefone und Radios waren damals noch relativ selten. Nachrichten und öffentliche Informationen wurden überwiegend durch die Wochenschauen in den Kinos verbreitet, die in der großen Zeit der Schwarzweißfilme sehr populär und gut besucht waren. In den meisten Wohnungen waren die Zimmer noch immer mit schweren Möbeln und dekorativem Nippes voll gestellt und mit mühsam zu befeuernden Holz- oder Kohleöfen zu heizen. Im Laufe der 20er Jahre setzten sich nachhaltig wichtige technische Neuerungen durch, sodass am Ende des Jahrzehnts sehr viel mehr Menschen Zugang zu elektrischem Strom, Autos und Radios hatten und eine kleine privilegierte Elite sich sogar den Luxus von Kühlschränken leisten konnte.

Trotz der voranschreitenden Entwicklung war dieses Jahrzehnt aber noch immer eine Zeit großer Entbehrungen. Als Folge des Ersten Weltkriegs bestand in den frühen 20er Jahren ein akuter Bedarf an Wohnungen und neuen Möbeln. Deutschland war durch die hohen Reparationszahlungen, die ihm im Frieden von Versailles auferlegt worden waren, völlig verarmt und erlebte zwischen 1922 und 1923 eine galoppierende Inflation, die durch die Ausgabe von Banknoten im Wert von über 1 Million Reichsmark weiter eskalierte und die Ersparnisse der Mittelschicht völlig aufzehrte. Vor diesem düsteren Hintergrund wirkt es geradezu paradox, dass Berlin die freizügigste und aufregendste Stadt Europas wurde. Seine berüchtigten Kabaretts waren für ihre intellektuelle Dekadenz berühmt und gaben der Stadt den Ruf eines »modernen Babylon«.

In den frühen 20er Jahren litt auch die britische Bevölkerung unter dramatischen Preissteigerungen, die durch Materialknappheit und einen Mangel an Arbeitskräften bedingt waren. Hinzu kam, dass die britische Regierung versuchte, die Beseitigung der Kriegsschäden durch Steuererhöhungen zu finanzieren. Diese Umverteilung der Einkommen veränderte die Lebensgewohnheiten aller Gesellschaftsschichten nachhaltig. Die Mangelerscheinungen und höheren Steuerbelastungen zwangen nicht nur Industrie und Handel, Betriebseinschränkungen und Entlassungen vorzunehmen, sondern auch die oberen Mittelschichten sahen sich nun gezwungen, nach kleineren, wirtschaftlicheren Häusern Ausschau zu halten. Der akute Mangel an Hauspersonal führte zu einer gesteigerten Nachfrage nach arbeitssparenden Haushaltsgeräten wie Waschmaschinen und Staubsaugern, um diese missliche Situation auszugleichen.

Da ihnen nun weniger Einkommen zur Verfügung stand, konnten die oberen Mittelschichten das Kunsthandwerk jetzt nicht mehr in dem gewohnten Maß unterstützen. Viele Produzenten spezialisierten sich deshalb auf die Herstellung geschmackvoller preiswerter Objekte mit einem universalen Appeal. Es lag auf der Hand, dass die große Nachfrage nach preiswerten Wohnungen und Möbeln nur befriedigt werden konnte, wenn die Architekten und Designer Standardisierung und industrielle Massenfertigung akzeptierten. Und obwohl die meisten Verbraucher die neuen, fortschrittlichen Haushaltsgeräte auch kauften, blieb der allgemeine Geschmack in großen Teilen der Bevölkerung doch eher ultra-konservativ. Die funktionale

Schlichtheit der modernen Ästhetik in der Architektur und im Möbeldesign konnte sich noch nicht allgemein durchsetzen. Trotzdem lassen sich in den Entwürfen für Wohnhäuser in den Vorstädten moderne Gestaltungsprinzipien nachweisen, die auf ältere Arbeiten von Architekten wie C. F. A. Voysey zurückgehen. Diese schlichten Bauten mit schmucklosen Fassaden waren, um Kosten zu sparen, als Bungalows konzipiert worden. In den frühen 20er Jahren waren Architektur und Design noch von national- und regionaltypischen Merkmalen geprägt. In Großbritannien zeigten sie nüchterne Schlichtheit und gute Verarbeitung, inspiriert waren sie von einheimischen Bauformen. Das französische Design war für hochkarätige luxuriöse und opulente Innenausstattungen berühmt, in Deutschland und Österreich war es eher klassisch, schwer und geometrisch. Der Internationale Stil wurde erst um 1927 als universale Formensprache des Funktionalismus von der Avantgarde allgemein akzeptiert.

Überschwang und Luxus

Zwar stellte auch *Decorative Art* in den späten 20er Jahren moderne Bauentwürfe vor, aber das waren seltene Ausnahmen. Denn in Großbritannien und in den Vereinigten Staaten bevorzugte das Gros der einflussreichen Bauherren weiterhin den Arts-and-Crafts- oder Art-déco-Stil. Der Begriff »Art déco« geht auf den Titel der Exposition Internationale des Arts Décoratifs et Industriels Modernes 1925 in Paris zurück und bezeichnet einen extravaganten luxuriösen Stil, der durch die Verwendung von exotischen Materialien wie Perlmutt, Schildpatt und Chagrinleder sowie durch strenge geometrische Formen gekennzeichnet ist. Im Gegensatz zum älteren Art nouveau, das von bodenständigen, natürlichen organischen Formen inspiriert war, griff der Art-déco-Stil auf eine Vielzahl von Quellen zurück, darunter die ägyptische und afrikanische Kunst, den Futurismus, Kubismus und Neoklassizismus und sogar die Moderne. Im Vergleich zu den nach dem Krieg von René Lalique produzierten schimmernden Art-déco-Gläsern, die auf maskulinen, kräftigen geometrischen Formen basieren, wirken die von Émile Gallé vor dem Krieg hergestellten Artnouveau-Kameogläser mit ihren floralen Motiven und wellenförmigen, organisch-fließenden Formen feminin und zart.

In der Mitte der 20er Jahre genoss das französische Design ein sehr hohes Ansehen, und die Avantgarde hatte sich in Paris konzentriert. Unterstützt und gefördert von einer wohlhabenden Kundschaft, zu der auch die Modeschöpfer Paul Poiret und Jacques Douce gehörten, ließen die berühmtesten Designer des kostspieligen Art-déco-Stils, Jacques-Émile Ruhlmann und Sue et Mare, die dekorativen Traditionen Frankreichs durch ihre meisterhafte Beherrschung der Handwerkstechniken und die Verarbeitung luxuriöser Materialien wieder aufleben. Durch seine enge Verbindung zur *Haute Couture* war das französische Art déco nicht nur extravagant und luxuriös, sondern auch außerordentlich einflussreich, und es inspirierte besonders die britischen und amerikanischen Designer bis weit in die 30er Jahre hinein. Ihre Entwürfe erreichten aber nur selten die hohe Qualität und die geschmackvolle Eleganz der frühen französischen Arbeiten. Designer wie Eileen Gray und Edgar Brandt, die in den späten 20er Jahren in Paris tätig waren, arbeiteten in einem Übergangsstil, der die Brücke vom Art déco zur Moderne schlug. In ihren klaren, sachlichen Entwürfen griffen sie zwar die Ästhetik der Moderne auf, blieben aber grundsätzlich noch dekorativ.

Die meisten Innenausstattungen der 20er Jahre waren noch immer verhältnismäßig ornamental, wobei modische Patchwork-Kissen und Textilapplikationen in leuchtenden Farben die notwendigen farbigen Akzente setzten. Auch die Wiener Werkstätte und Foxton in London produzierten Stoffe mit leuchtenden Farben und oft abstrakten floralen Mustern. Kühne Farbkombinationen, die von der zeitgenössischen Kunst inspiriert waren, wie Ultramarine-Schwarz oder Schwarz-Weiß, kamen in Mode, und exzentrische geometrische Formen beherrschten die Entwürfe. Die Reformer unter den Designern lehnten Tendenzen im Art déco ab, bei denen »Originalität um der Originalität willen« angestrebt wurde. Dieser ästhetizistische Stil war ungeeignet für die industrielle Produktion, beeinflusste aber den Massengeschmack durch die stilvolle Eleganz, die mit ihm assoziiert wurde.

Im Gegensatz zu Europa erlebten die Vereinigten Staaten nach dem Ersten Weltkrieg einen außergewöhnlichen wirtschaftlichen Aufschwung. In den 20er Jahren hütete Amerika die größten Goldreserven der Welt, seine Bürger genossen größere Freiheiten und einen nie gekannten Wohlstand. Der »American Dream«, das alles beherrschende Leitmotiv dieser Zeit, manifestierte sich besonders in New York und Chicago im Bau riesiger, hoch aufragender Wolkenkratzer, die zu den unbestrittenen technischen Wunderwerken ihrer Zeit gehörten. Der Geist des Jazz-Zeitalters fand seinen vollkommensten Ausdruck in dem überwältigenden Chrysler Building (1928–1930) in New York. Dieser elegante Art-déco-Bau, den Wilhelm van Alen entworfen hatte, wurde zum prägnantesten Symbol des aufstrebenden Amerika – und er war die Antithese aller Ideale, für die sich die europäische Avantgarde einsetzte. Der Modern Style – eine Variante des Art déco, die stilistisch von der avantgardistischen Moderne inspiriert war – erlebte seine Blütezeit in den Vereinigten Staaten in den späten 20er und frühen 30er Jahren. Hollywoods Filmausstatter verhalfen auch dem Modern Style, der sich durch Glas und glänzende Chromflächen auszeichnete, zu allgemeiner Akzeptanz und Popularität.

Form follows Function

Zwischen 1914 und 1920 waren in Großbritannien die Baukosten um ca. 400 % gestiegen. Um den immer größer werdenden Bedarf an zweckmäßigen und preiswerten Wohnungen zu befriedigen, wurde Beton als Baumaterial eingeführt. Er eignete sich hervorragend zur Errichtung von Bogenkonstruktionen, die wirtschaftlicher waren als die Holzträger, die man traditionell beim Bau von Backsteinhäusern verwendet hatte. Bogenstellungen aus Beton waren in ihrer Struktur belastbarer und benötigten 50–100 % weniger Material. Zu den weiteren Vorteilen des Betons zählte, dass er feuer- und wetterfest und leicht zu pflegen war und den Architekten größere Ausdrucksmöglichkeiten bot, da er nicht den gleichen physikalischen Einschränkungen wie Holz, Stein oder Backstein unterlag. Bis 1920 waren zwar nur wenige Bauvorhaben in dem aufregenden neuen Material realisiert worden, aber am Ende der Dekade war Beton zum bevorzugten Baumaterial der Architekten der Moderne avanciert.

Der Reformbewegung der Moderne ging es nicht nur um progressives Design, sondern auch um soziale Anliegen. Vereinigungen wie der Deutsche Werkbund und Publikationen wie *Decorative Art* setzten sich mit großem Eifer für eine allgemeine Verbreitung des Funktionalismus ein. In der Geschichte der Moderne war die Bauhaus-Ausstel-lung von 1923 in Weimar der entscheidende Wendepunkt, denn sie brachte der neuen Bewegung die erste internationale Anerkennung. Ihre Vertreter in Deutschland, Holland, Frankreich und Großbritannien, unter ihnen Walter Gropius, Marcel Breuer, Gerrit Rietveld, J. J. P. Oud, Le Corbusier, Charlotte Perriand und Ambrose Heal, wandten sich als Pioniere eines neuen Stils in Architektur und Design ganz entschieden gegen den verschwenderischen Überfluss des zeitgenössischen Art-déco-Stils. Ihre klaren, funktionalen Entwürfe entsprachen der Maxime des amerikanischen Architekten Louis H. Sullivan, »form follows function«. Häuser wurden als »Wohnmaschinen« konzipiert und Möbel als »Ausrüstungen zum Leben«. Mit neuen Materialien (Beton, Spiegelglas, Stahlrohr) und innovativen Produktionsverfahren entwickelten die Designer und Architekten der Moderne mit ihren Bauten und Innenausstattungen ein formales Vokabular, das der klassischen Geometrie (Quadrat, Kubus, Kreis, Zylinder, Kegel und Dreieck) entnommen und zukunftsorientiert war. Auch in der Keramik setzten sich schlichte, schmucklose Formen durch, die sich deutlich vom üppigen traditionellen lithographischen Transferdruck der viktorianischen Zeit unterschieden.

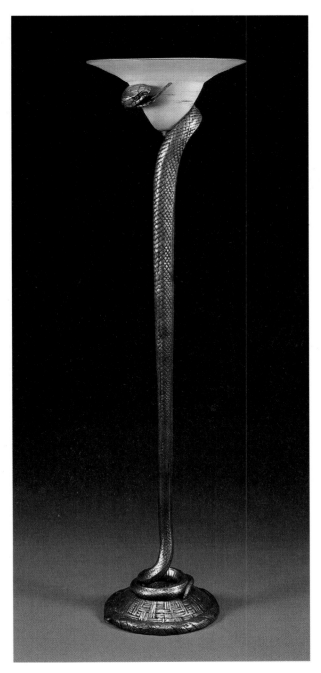

Die Vertreter der Moderne versuchten, Schönheit mit Zweck- und Nützlichkeitsaspekten zu verbinden. Ihre Entwürfe für Gegenstände des täglichen Gebrauchs und Möbel, wie der allgegenwärtige Stuhl aus Stahlrohr, sollten in harmonischem Einklang mit den Bedürfnissen des 20. Jahrhunderts stehen und für industrielle Herstellungsverfahren geeignet sein. Mechanisierung war die Realität, wie Shirley Wainwright feststellte, als sie 1923 in *Decorative Art* schrieb: »Die Lebensbedürfnisse der breiten Öffentlichkeit werden durch industrielle Produktionsverfahren befriedigt, auf Maschinen kann nicht mehr verzichtet werden. Deshalb müssen alle wirklich konstruktiven Beiträge zum Nutzen der industriellen Kunst in Zukunft diese Tatsache ehrlich anerkennen. Die zukünftige Entwicklung der angewandten Kunst wird sicherlich demokratische Tendenzen haben.« Die Vertreter der Moderne bemühten sich, der billigen Fabrikware und dem Kitsch formschöne Industrieprodukte von hoher Qualität entgegenzusetzen. *Decorative Art* empfahl, in jedem Haus eine kleine »Schreckenskammer« für Gegenstände und Möbel einzurichten, die nicht mehr zeitgemäß seien, von denen man sich emotional aber noch nicht trennen könne. Das Gestaltungsprinzip »Kunst um der Kunst willen« wurde durch eine Kunstethik ersetzt, die dem Wohl der Gesellschaft verpflichtet war. Auch schlagkräftige Werbekampagnen trugen dazu bei, dass sich modernes Design allgemein durchsetzte. Die Verbraucher verlangten zunehmend nach Eigenschaften wie Angemessenheit, Zweckmäßigkeit und Schönheit für die Gegenstände des täglichen Bedarfs. In der Mitte der 20er Jahre setzte sich – insbesondere in Frankreich und Deutschland – auch bei den Unternehmern die Einsicht durch, dass gutes Design auch gute Profite bringt. Viele etablierte Hersteller begannen ihre Produktion auf qualitätvolles modernes Industriedesign umzustellen. Selbst in Großbritannien und in den Vereinigten Staaten wurde es nicht nur von einer neuen Generation von Architekten und Designern, sondern auch von den Verbrauchern aller Altersgruppen allgemein enthusiastisch akzeptiert.

1927 veranstaltete der Deutsche Werkbund in Stuttgart die einzigartige Ausstellung »Die Wohnung«. Mies van der Rohe, der sie organisierte, hatte die fortschrittlichsten Architekten Europas eingeladen, sich an diesem Wettbewerb in der Weißenhofsiedlung zu beteiligen. Die Häuser und Wohnungseinrichtungen mit Möbeln von Mart Stam, Marcel Breuer und Le Corbusier, um nur einige zu nennen, wurden ausführlich publiziert und auch in das *Decorative Art*-Jahrbuch 1929 aufgenommen. Diese Ausstellung führte zu einer breiten Akzeptanz der Moderne, die sich im folgenden Jahrzehnt zu einem wahrhaft internationalen Stil entwickelte. Insofern sie Gebäude und Objekte eher unter wissenschaftlich-mathematischen als künstlerisch-emotionalen Gesichtspunkten konzipierten, reduzierten Architekten der Moderne, wie Le Corbusier oder Walter Gropius, die Architektur und das Design zu einer formalen Aufgabe. Die von ihnen verwirklichten Bauten mit leichten Stahlrahmen, Stahlbeton und großen Verglasungen hatten oft einen eher sterilen als wohnlichen Charakter und boten Funktionalität ohne übermäßigen Wohnkomfort. Das von den Architekten der Moderne konzipierte Haus der Zukunft mit zweckmäßig ausgestatteten Küchen und Einbauschränken benötigte kaum Möbel und war durch Symmetrie, Klarheit und Helligkeit gekennzeichnet. Das bescheidene Heim schien endlich zu einem wirklichen Industrieprodukt umgestaltet worden zu sein.

INTRODUCTION
LES ANNÉES 20

Reconstruction, industrialisation et standardisation

Les années 20 furent des années d'optimisme au cours desquelles tous les regards étaient tournés vers l'avenir et où chacun plaçait sa confiance et ses espoirs dans le progrès technologique. Le carnage de la Grande Guerre avait irrévocablement transformé la société mais eut également pour effet d'accélérer la transition de l'ère édouardienne aux temps modernes. Au début de la décennie, les automobiles se partageaient encore les routes avec les voitures à chevaux et, bien que les rues soient déjà éclairées à l'électricité, la majorité des foyers utilisaient encore des lampes à gaz ou à huile. La plupart possédaient un gramophone, mais les téléphones et les postes de T. S. F. étaient encore relativement rares. Les nouvelles et les informations publiques se transmettaient en grande partie grâce aux actualités projetées dans les salles de cinéma, qui, naturellement, étaient surtout populaires pour leurs films en noir et blanc. Les maisons, souvent encombrées de meubles imposants

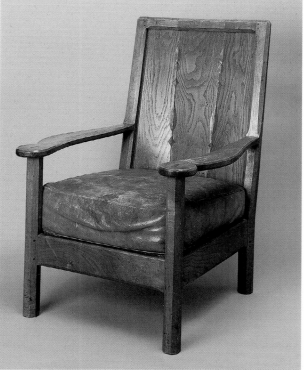

et d'objets décoratifs, étaient chauffées par des poêles à charbon ou à bois qui exigeaient un entretien laborieux. Cependant, d'immenses avancées technologiques apparurent tout au long de la décennie. Vers la fin des années 20, le nombre de personnes ayant accès à l'électricité, à l'automobile et à la T. S. F. avait considérablement augmenté, tandis qu'une poignée de privilégiés jouissaient même du luxe d'un réfrigérateur.

Ce fut néanmoins une décennie très éprouvante. Le début des années 20 fut marqué par une grave pénurie de logements et un manque de nouveau mobilier. Entre 1922 et 1923, l'Allemagne, déjà très appauvrie par les réparations que lui imposaient l'Armistice et le traité de Versailles, se retrouva aux prises avec l'hyperinflation. Celle-ci culmina avec l'édition de billets de banque atteignant jusqu'à un million de Reichsmarks et réduisant à néant l'épargne des classes moyennes. Paradoxalement, en dépit de la misère ambiante, Berlin devint la capitale la plus permissive et affriolante d'Europe. Ses fameux cabarets célébraient une décadence grisante qui donna à la ville sa réputation de « Babylone des temps modernes ».

En Grande-Bretagne, la population fut également durement touchée par une hausse vertigineuse des prix, conséquence de la pénurie de matières premières et de main-d'œuvre. Le gouvernement augmenta également les impôts pour aider à rembourser les frais de guerre. La redistribution des richesses eut un impact considérable sur les trains de vie de toutes les couches de la société. Tandis que la situation économique forçait les entreprises à réduire leur taille, la haute bourgeoisie, désormais moins prospère car plus lourdement imposée, commença à se rendre compte qu'il lui fallait des maisons moins grandes et mieux agencées. Au cours de cette période, le manque de personnel de maison entraîna une très forte demande d'ap-

pareils ménagers tels que des machines à laver le linge ou des aspirateurs, ce qui contribua largement à compenser le manque de domestiques.

Avec moins de revenus à sa disposition, la haute bourgeoisie n'avait plus les moyens de financer les arts décoratifs autant que par le passé. De ce fait, de nombreux créateurs se concentrèrent sur un design plus démocratique et moins cher, capable d'exercer un attrait universel. Dans le domaine de l'architecture, il était évident que l'énorme demande de l'après-guerre en logements et meubles abordables ne pourrait être satisfaite que si les architectes et les designers adoptaient l'industrialisation et la standardisation. Mais si le public était prêt à accepter de nouveaux appareils ménagers futuristes, il conservait, dans sa grande majorité, un goût ultra-conservateur et était nettement moins enclin à accepter l'esthétique sobre du modernisme lorsque celui-ci était appliqué à l'architecture ou à la décoration d'intérieur. L'émergence d'un Modern Style était néanmoins déjà perceptible dans les banlieues, où les nouvelles constructions étaient souvent influencées par les travaux antérieurs d'architectes tels que Charles Voysey. Ces pavillons avaient souvent des façades sans ornement et ne comportaient pas d'étages afin de limiter les coûts. Au début des années 20, le design était encore marqué par de fortes caractéristiques nationales et régionales. Le design britannique était simple, austère, bien fait et adapté à son contexte ; le français était de haute qualité, luxueux et opulent ; l'allemand et l'autrichien classiques, lourds et géométriques. Il fallut attendre 1927 pour que le style international fasse son apparition et que le langage universel du fonctionnalisme domine l'avant-garde.

Luxe et exubérance

Les bâtiments modernistes présentés dans les annuaires de *Decorative Art* à la fin des années 20 étaient des exemples très rares. La plupart des riches clients d'architectes, notamment en Grande-Bretagne et aux Etats-Unis, continuèrent à leur préférer les styles Arts & Crafts ou Art Déco. Le terme Art Déco venait du titre d'une exposition orga-

nisée à Paris en 1925, *L'Exposition Internationale des Arts Décoratifs et Industriels Modernes.* On y présentait un style luxueux et sophistiqué, caractérisé par le recours à des matériaux exotiques tels que la nacre et le galuchat, ainsi que par des formes géométriques audacieuses. Contrairement au style Art nouveau qui l'avait précédé en s'inspirant de l'environnement et de formes organiques naturelles, l'Art Déco puisait dans un éventail éclectique de sources comprenant l'art égyptien et africain, le futurisme, le cubisme, le néoclassicisme et même le modernisme. Comparés aux verreries opalescentes de l'après-guerre de René Lalique, qui jouait sur la notion de volume et se basait sur des formes géométriques puissantes, les vases irisés produits au début du siècle par Emile Gallé, avec leurs motifs floraux et leurs formes organiques douces et sinueuses, paraissaient très délicats et féminins.

Au milieu des années 20, le design français occupa le devant de la scène, l'avant-garde étant principalement concentrée à Paris. Encouragés par le mécénat d'une clientèle riche, dont les couturiers Paul Poiret et Jacques Doucet, les plus grands représentants du style Art Déco, tels que Jacques-Emile Ruhlman ou le duo André Mare et Louis Sue, firent revivre la tradition française du *décorateur* par leur talent artisanal exceptionnel et le recours à des matériaux nobles. Fortement associé à la haute couture, l'Art Déco français, à la fois extravagant et luxueux, avait une très grand influence. Il continua à inspirer les créateurs anglais et américains tout au long des années 30, mais rares furent ceux qui parvinrent à égaler la haute qualité d'exécution et le brio des premières créations françaises. D'autres designers actifs à la fin des années 20, comme Eileen Gray et Edgar Brandt, travaillaient dans un style à mi-chemin entre l'Art Déco et le modernisme. Leurs créations audacieuses empruntaient à l'esthétique de ce dernier tout en restant fondamentalement décoratives.

Dans les années 20, la majorité des intérieurs faisaient la part belle à la décoration, la mode des coussins en patchwork et des applications sur tissu apportant aux foyers les touches de couleurs vives dont ils avaient tant besoin. Les étoffes fabriquées par Wiener Werkstätte à Vienne et Foxtons à Londres étaient également vivement colorées et présentaient souvent des motifs floraux abstraits. Les combinaisons de couleurs audacieuses inspirées par la peinture contemporaine, tels que noir et outremer ou blanc et noir,

devinrent de plus en plus prisées, tout comme les formes géométriques excentriques qui présentaient souvent un aspect bizarre. Les réformateurs du design s'insurgeaient contre cette tendance de l'Art Déco à rechercher l'originalité à tout prix, mais le style, qui avait peu de choses à voir avec la production industrielle, parvint à influencer le goût du grand public par ses connotations de sophistication et de luxe.

Contrairement à l'Europe, les Etats-Unis de l'après-guerre connurent une période de grande prospérité. Au début des années 20, ils avaient amassé la plus grande réserve d'or au monde et leurs habitants jouissaient d'une liberté et d'une richesse sans précédent. On poursuivait la notion du « rêve américain » sans relâche, celui-ci étant symbolisé au mieux par la construction de gratte-ciel massifs, notamment à New York et à Chicago qui rivalisaient en prouesses techniques. L'esprit du « Jazz Age » trouva une expression sans pareille avec le Chrysler Building (1928–1930) construit à New York par William van Alen. Cet exubérant bâtiment Art Déco devint le totem de l'Amérique capitaliste en plein boom, l'antithèse de tout ce que l'avant-garde européenne incarnait à l'époque. Le Modern Style, une forme d'Art Déco qui, sur le plan stylistique, s'inspirait du modernisme, s'épanouit également aux Etats-Unis entre la fin des années 20 et le début des années 30. Comme pour l'Art Déco, les décors des films hollywoodiens aidèrent à populariser ce style, qui se distinguait le plus souvent par le recours au verre et à un chrome étincelant.

La forme suit la fonction

Entre 1914 et 1920, le coût de la construction en Grande-Bretagne s'éleva de près de 400 %. Le besoin de bâtiments meilleur marché et plus efficaces qui s'ensuivit entraîna l'introduction du béton, bien adapté aux constructions voûtées : pour soutenir de lourdes charges, il était en effet plus économique que les poutres en bois utilisées traditionnellement dans les maisons en briques. Les bâtiments voûtés n'étaient pas seulement plus solides structurellement, ils nécessitaient également 50 à 100% de matériaux en moins. En outre, le béton présentait l'avantage de résister aux incendies, aux intempéries et de ne nécessiter pratiquement aucun entretien. Parce qu'il n'était pas soumis aux mêmes contraintes physiques que le bois, la pierre ou la brique, il offrait aussi un plus grand potentiel expressif aux architectes. En 1920, il n'existait encore que quelques bâtiments réalisés dans ce matériau nouveau et passionnant, mais vers la fin de la décennie, il avait été adopté par la plupart des architectes associés au mouvement moderne.

Les modernistes considéraient la réforme du design comme une nécessité. Des organisations telles que le Deutscher Werkbund ainsi que des publications comme les annuaires de *Decorative Art* défendaient sans relâche la cause fonctionnaliste. L'exposition du Bauhaus de 1923 marqua sans doute le virage le plus déterminant dans l'histoire du design moderne car, pour la première fois, elle attira l'attention d'un vaste public international sur ce nouveau courant. Les designers du mouvement moderne d'Allemagne, de Hollande, de France et de Grande-Bretagne,

dont Walter Gropius, Marcel Breuer, Gerrit Rietveld, J. J. P. Oud, Le Corbusier, Charlotte Perriand et Ambrose Heal, présentaient tous une nouvelle approche de l'architecture et du design qui s'opposait radicalement aux excès décoratifs de l'Art Déco contemporain. Leurs créations se caractérisaient par une simplicité austère et utilitaire, fidèle à la formule de l'architecte américain Louis H. Sullivan (1856–1924) : « La forme suit la fonction ». Les maisons devinrent des « machines pour vivre » tandis que les meubles étaient conçus comme « un équipement pour vivre ». Adoptant les nouveaux matériaux (béton, plaques de verre, métal tubulaire) et les méthodes innovatrices de production désormais disponibles, ils créèrent des bâtiments et des objets qui possédaient un vocabulaire formel basé sur la géométrie classique (le carré, le cube, le cercle, le cylindre, le cône et le triangle) et qui étaient tournés vers l'avenir. Les cérami-

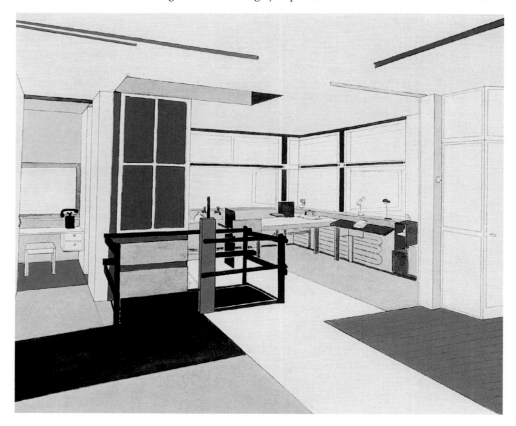

ques, par exemple, avaient désormais des formes simples et nues qui contrastaient nettement avec le clinquant des transferts de lithographie de l'époque victorienne.

Les acteurs du modernisme voulaient des objets utilitaires et beaux qui soient dépouillés de tout ornement futile. Leurs meubles, tel que le fameux fauteuil à armature métallique tubulaire, se voulaient en accord avec les modes de vie du 20e siècle comme avec les méthodes de fabrication modernes. La mécanisation était la nouvelle réalité, comme le déclara Shirley Wainwright en 1923 dans *Decorative Art*: «En ce qui concerne les besoins généraux du public, les machines dominent entièrement la production et sont maintenant indispensables. A l'avenir, les contributions les plus précieuses à la bonne santé de l'art industriel devront être fondées sur une reconnaissance directe de cet état de fait. Les nouvelles tendances dans les arts appliqués

auront inévitablement des penchants démocratiques». Les modernistes pensaient pouvoir supplanter la pléthore de produits de mauvaise qualité et souvent kitsch grâce à leur design démocratique intègre produit industriellement. Les annuaires conseillaient même à chaque foyer de convertir une petite pièce en «chambre des horreurs» pour y stocker tous les objets désuets auxquels on attachait une valeur sentimentale. «L'art pour l'art» était à présent remplacé par «l'art pour la société». Par la force de la publicité, le grand public devint de plus en plus réceptif au design moderne et exigea de plus en plus «aptitude, utilité et beauté» pour les objets dont il s'entourait. Vers le milieu des années 20, on comprit, notamment en France et en Allemagne, que le bon design était rentable et de nombreux fabricants établis se mirent à produire des objets résolument modernistes. Même en Grande-Bretagne et aux Etats-Unis,

le design moderne était considéré comme une évolution nécessaire et logique et ce, non plus uniquement par une génération prometteuse d'architectes et de designers mais par des amateurs de tous âges.

En 1927 à Stuttgart, le Deutscher Werkbund organisa une exposition exceptionnelle intitulée *Die Wohnung* (l'habitation) sous la baguette de Ludwig Mies van der Rohe. Elle était centrée sur un projet d'habitations à loyers modérés pour lequel les architectes les plus progressistes d'Europe étaient invités à concevoir des bâtiments. Les maisons et leurs intérieurs, meublés de créations conçues par Mart Stam, Marcel Breuer et Le Corbusier pour n'en citer que quelques-uns, furent l'objet d'une très large publicité et on les présenta dans l'annuaire de 1929 de *Decorative Art*. Cette exposition entraîna une plus grande acceptation du modernisme qui, au cours de la décennie suivante, devait devenir un style véritablement international. Cependant, en concevant des bâtiments et des objets d'une manière scientifique et mathématique plutôt qu'artistique et émotionnelle, les architectes associés au mouvement moderne

tels que Le Corbusier ou Walter Gropius réduisirent l'architecture et le design à la mise en pratique d'une formule. Les bâtiments qu'ils créaient avec des structures métalliques légères, des murs en béton armé et des cloisons en panneaux de verre avaient un caractère stérile plutôt qu'accueillant et leur fonctionnalisme était assez dénué de chaleur humaine. Les maisons du futur pour les modernistes, avec leurs cuisines laboratoires et leurs placards intégrés, nécessitaient peu de meubles et se caractérisaient par leur symétrie, leur lumière et leur propreté. L'humble demeure, semblait-il, avait finalement été transfigurée en un parfait produit industrialisé.

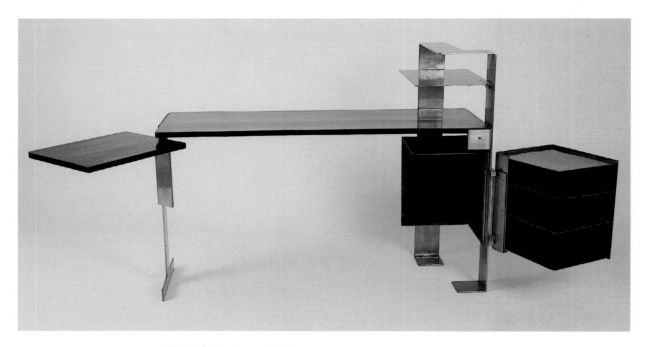

architecture and interiors | Architektur und Interieurs | Architecture et intérieurs

DECORATIVE SCHEME FOR A DINING-ROOM, WITH PAINTED WOODWORK
by Shirley B. Wainwright

DECORATIVE SCHEME FOR A DINING-ROOM
by Shirley B. Wainwright

GROUP OF DINING-ROOM FURNITURE

by Shirley B. Wainwright

SIMPLE TREATMENT OF A SMALL BEDROOM
by Shirley B. Wainwright

SUGGESTED TREATMENT OF A SITTING-ROOM
by Shirley B. Wainwright

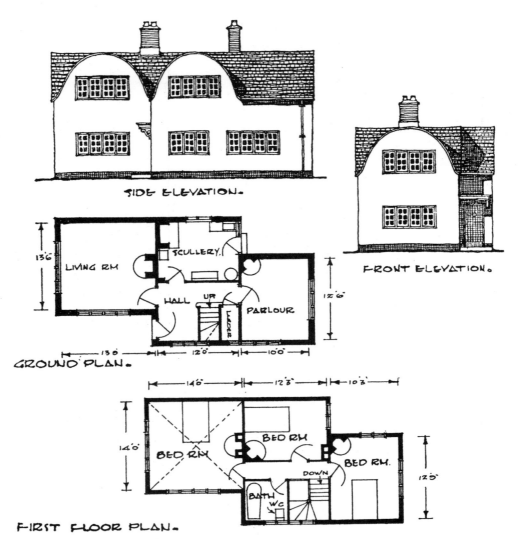

SIDE ELEVATION.

FRONT ELEVATION.

GROUND PLAN.

LIVING RM

SCULLERY.

HALL

UP

PARLOUR

13'6

13'0

12'0

10'0

12'6

FIRST FLOOR PLAN.

BED RM

BED RM

BED RM

BATH

WC

DOWN

14'0

14'0

12'3

10'3

12'5

PROPOSED COTTAGE AT MUSWELL HILL

MAURICE S. R. ADAMS, A.R.I.B.A., ARCHITECT

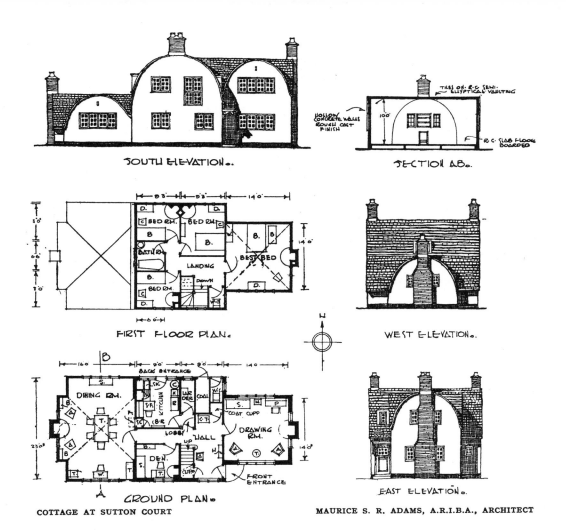

SOUTH ELEVATION.

SECTION AB.

FIRST FLOOR PLAN.

WEST ELEVATION.

GROUND PLAN.

EAST ELEVATION.

COTTAGE AT SUTTON COURT

MAURICE S. R. ADAMS, A.R.I.B.A., ARCHITECT

PAINTED FURNITURE DESIGNED AND EXECUTED BY CARL MALMSTEN

LIVING-ROOM DESIGNED BY E. G. ASPLUND

LIVING-ROOM DESIGNED AND EXECUTED BY THE NORDISKA KOMPANIET

ROOM IN THE LAW COURTS, STOCKHOLM. CARL WESTMAN, ARCHITECT

HOUSE NEAR NEW YORK.   DWIGHT
JAMES BAUM, ARCHITECT

VILLA AT SOUTHAMPTON, L.I.
WALKER & GILLETTE, ARCHITECTS

VILLA AT SOUTHAMPTON, L.I. WALKER & GILLETTE, ARCHITECTS

A DANISH SUMMER RESIDENCE
LOUIS HYGOM, ARCHITECT

HOUSE AT NÄRUM, DENMARK
LOUIS   HYGOM,   ARCHITECT

.FRONT ELEVATION.

.GARDEN ELEVATION.

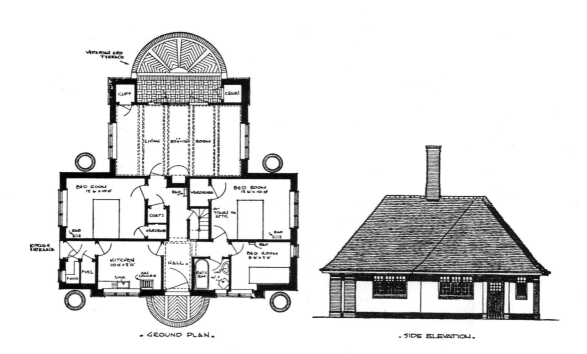

.GROUND PLAN.

.SIDE ELEVATION.

PROPOSED BUNGALOW AT CARDIFF.   MAURICE
S. R. ADAMS, A.R.I.B.A., ARCHITECT

THE ROEHAMPTON ESTATE

INFANTS SCHOOL & ROEHAMPTON

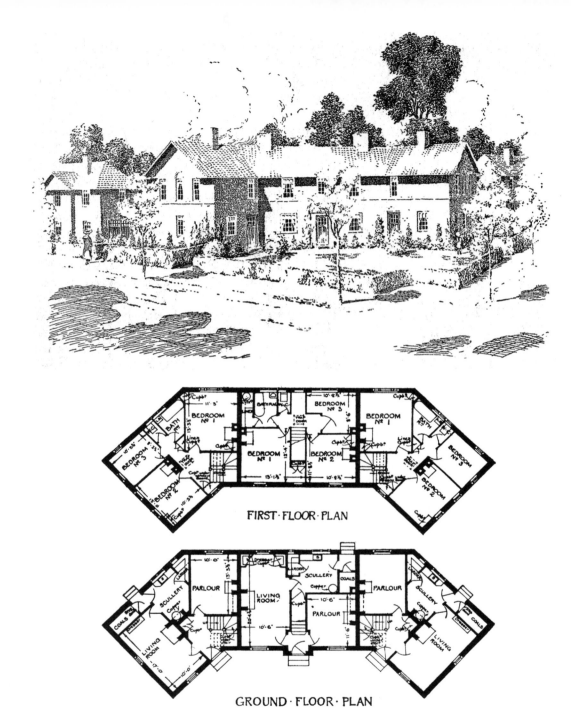

FIRST · FLOOR · PLAN

GROUND · FLOOR · PLAN

VIEW AT CROSSING, DOVER HOUSE ROAD AND HUNTINGFIELD ROAD.   BLOCK OF THREE FIVE-ROOMED HOUSES
The Roehampton Estate

VIEW TOWARDS SWINBURNE
ROAD FROM GIBBON WALK
The Roehampton Estate

BIRCHWOOD ARMCHAIR AND SIDE-TABLE
DESIGNED AND EXECUTED BY CHR. RASCH

WRITING-ROOM AND LIBRARY DESIGNED BY HUGO GORGE, VIENNA
EXECUTED BY KUNST UND WOHNUNG R. LORENZ, VIENNA

GROUPS OF HOUSES AT STOCKHOLM

HOUSE AT STOCKHOLM.   ARCHITECT, PROF. IVAR TENGBOM

"VIRGINIA," VANCLUSE, SYDNEY, AUSTRALIA
THE LOGGIA. ARCHITECT, H. C. DAY, SYDNEY

HOUSE IN FLEMISH STYLE AT KNOCKE, BELGIUM.   ARCHITECT, ADOLPHE PIRENNE, S.C.A.B., BRUSSELS

HOUSE AT CARTIGNY, GENEVA.   ARCHITECT, G. REVILLIOD, GENEVA.

HOUSE AT MORGAT. ARCHITECT, G. C. CHABAL, BREST

WORKMEN'S DWELLINGS AT BRUSSELS
ARCHITECT, JOSEPH DIONGRE, BRUSSELS

Materials: Foundations in stone, lower portion of walls faced with coloured cement, upper portion in brick

HOUSE AT MORGAT. ARCHITECT, G. C. CHABAL, BREST

DESIGNS FOR COUNTRY HOUSES
BY LOUIS MAS, ARCHITECT, PARIS

DESIGN FOR A COUNTRY HOUSE, BY H. REDARD (DOMINIQUE), ARCHITECT, PARIS

MODEL FOR A COUNTRY HOUSE IN THE SOUTH OF FRANCE, BY ROB MALLET-STEVENS, ARCHITECT, PARIS

" CRABBY CORNER," LETCHWORTH, HERTS.—THE
DRAWING-ROOM. ARCHITECT, BARRY PARKER
F.R.I.B.A., LETCHWORTH, WHO ALSO DESIGNED
THE FURNITURE

"WHIRRIESTONE," NEAR ROCHDALE—THE DINING-ROOM.   ARCHITECT, BARRY PARKER, F.R.I.B.A., LETCHWORTH, WHO ALSO DESIGNED THE FURNITURE, CARPET, FITTINGS, ETC.

"CRABBY CORNER," LETCHWORTH, HERTS.—A BEDROOM. ARCHITECT, BARRY PARKER, F.R.I.B.A., LETCHWORTH

DAY NURSERY SHOWN BY THE LONDON GAS EXHIBIT COMMITTEE AT THE WOMAN'S EXHIBITION. ARCHITECT H. AUSTEN HALL, F.R.I.B.A., 6, NEW BURLINGTON STREET, LONDON. FURNITURE AND DECORATION BY HEAL AND SON, LTD. BATHROOM FITTINGS BY DAVIS, BENNETT AND CO.

INTERIOR DESIGNED BY ROBERT MALLET-STEVENS, ARCHITECT, PARIS

BEDROOM WITH LIMEWOOD FURNITURE ORNAMENTED IN PEWTER AND IVORY
DESIGNED AND EXECUTED BY " MAM " (MICHEL DUFET AND LOUIS BUREAU), PARIS

BATHROOM DESIGNED AND EXECUTED BY LOUIS SUE ET
MARE, COMPAGNIE DES ARTS FRANCAIS, PARIS

DINING-ROOM DESIGNED BY ROBERT MALLET-STEVENS, ARCHITECT, PARIS

BATHROOOM DESIGNED AND EXECUTED BY "MARTINE," PARIS

INTERIOR ARRANGED BY ROBERT MALLET-STEVENS, ARCHITECT, PARIS

INTERIORS DESIGNED BY HUGO GORGE, VIENNA, EXECUTED
BY KUNST UND WOHNUNG R. LORENZ, VIENNA

INTERIOR DESIGNED BY HUGO GORGE, VIENNA, SHOWING
SIDEBOARD IN OLD PEASANT STYLE. EXECUTED BY
KUNST UND WOHNUNG R. LORENZ, VIENNA

I COUNTRY BRIDGE IN THE GARDEN OF BARON IWASAKI'S VILLA AT FUKAGAW, TOKYO; II ON AN
ISLAND IN THE SAME GARDEN, SHOWING A " YUKIMI TORO " UNDER A LEANING PINE TREE; III A CORNER
OF BARON IWASAKI'S GARDEN, SHOWING STEPPING-STONES, A FENCE AND A STONE LANTERN OF MIYA-
DACHI SHAPE; IV TEMPLE GARDEN AT UJI, SHOWING STONE BRIDGE AND LANTERNS

I COUNTRY BRIDGE IN THE GARDEN OF BARON IWASAKI'S VILLA AT FUKAGAW, TOKYO; II ON AN
ISLAND IN THE SAME GARDEN, SHOWING A " YUKIMI TORO " UNDER A LEANING PINE TREE; III A CORNER
OF BARON IWASAKI'S GARDEN, SHOWING STEPPING-STONES, A FENCE AND A STONE LANTERN OF MIYA-
DACHI SHAPE; IV TEMPLE GARDEN AT UJI, SHOWING STONE BRIDGE AND LANTERNS

STONE BASIN IN MR. NAKAI'S GARDEN, NAGOYA

A STONE LANTERN OF AN UNUSUAL SHAPE IN VISCOUNT MATSUURA'S GARDEN IN TOKIO

STONE LANTERN AND HISTORIC GATEWAY IN VISCOUNT MATSUURA'S GARDEN IN TOKIO

ENTRANCE TO MR. MIYAZAKI'S HOUSE IN NAGOYA, JAPAN

JAPANESE GARDEN IN THE KOISHIKAWA BOTANICAL GARDEN, TOKIO

ONE OF THE " SIX FLAT " GROUPS AND NEW HOUSES FOR THE TORONTO HOUSING COMPANY.   ARCHITECT,
F. H MARANI, TORONTO

HOUSE NEAR TORONTO.   ARCHITECT, F. H. MARANI,
TORONTO

HOUSE AT WESTMOUNT, NR. MONTREAL, RESIDENCE OF
THE ARCHITECT, FRANK R. FINDLAY, MONTREAL

SMALL HOUSE AT EDMONTON, ALBERTA. ARCHITECT, W. D. CROMARTY

LOGHOUSE AT SAHTLAM, VANCOUVER ISLAND, B.C. VIEW OF FRONT
AND PLAN. ARCHITECT, HUBERT SAVAGE, A.R.I.B.A., M.R.A.I.C.,
VICTORIA, B.C.

THREE HOUSES AT STRATFORD-UPON-AVON, "AVON MEAD," "AVON HOUSE," AND THE RESIDENCE OF THE ARCHITECT, L. L. DUSSAULT, F.R.I.B.A., 1, SALISBURY SQUARE, LONDON.

HOUSE AT CHIGWELL, ESSEX.
FROM A COLOURED DRAWING
BY THE ARCHITECT, SYDNEY
E. CASTLE, 40, ALBEMARLE
STREET, PICCADILLY, LONDON

RESIDENCE IN WUERBENTHAL. ARCHITECT, JOSEF HOFFMANN, VIENNA

COUNTRY HOUSE IN WINKELSDORF. ARCHITECT,
JOSEF HOFFMANN, VIENNA

RESIDENCE IN VIENNA—GARDEN ASPECT. ARCHITECTS,
F. KAYM AND A. HETMANEK, VIENNA

HOUSE AT WESTEND, BERLIN—FRONT ELEVATION.   ARCHITECT, DR. PAUL ZUCKER, BERLIN
Grey distemper; windows and ironwork red

TIMBER-BUILT HOUSE AT HELLERAU-DRESDEN.   ARCHITECT, KARL SCHMIDT

HOUSE IN ESSEX. INTERIOR
WITH A NORTHERLY ASPECT.
FROM A DRAWING BY DORA STONE

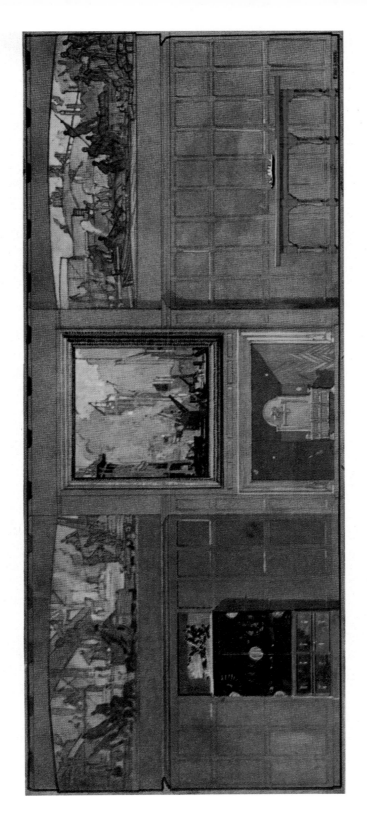

LINE WASHED OAK PANELLING SURMOUNTED WITH A PAINTED FRIEZE. DECORATION FOR THE BOARD ROOM OF A COLLIERY COMPANY. DESIGNED BY H. DAVIS RICHTER, R.I., R.O.I.

HOUSE AT RIVERSIDE, CONNECTICUT, U.S.A.   ARCHITECT, FRANK J. FORSTER
Built of fieldstone; slate roof

HOUSE AT CORNWALL, CONNECTICUT, U.S.A.   ARCHITECT, EDWARD C. DEAN

HOUSE AT RIVERSIDE, CONNECTICUT,
U.S.A. ARCHITECT, FRANK J. FORSTER
Built of Fieldstone; slate roof

HOUSE IN FREUDENTHAL—THE HALL.   ARCHITECT, PROF. JOSEF HOFFMANN, VIENNA

COUNTRY HOUSE, WINKELSDORF.   ARCHITECT, JOSEF
HOFFMANN, VIENNA

LIBRARY IN WALNUT, WITH BUILT-IN WRITING FLAP.
EXECUTED BY KARL SCHREITH. ARCHITECTS, K. HOFMANN
AND F. AUGENFELD, VIENNA

HOUSE IN FREUDENTHAL—THE DINING-ROOM. ARCHITECT, JOSEF HOFFMANN, VIENNA

CORNER OF LIBRARY IN A VIENNESE FLAT. WOODWORK IN WALNUT, EXECUTED BY KARL SCHREITH. ARCHITECTS,
KARL HOFMANN AND FELIX AUGENFELD, VIENNA

"VILLA FRIEDENSTEIN," VIENNA—LIBRARY AND DINING-ROOM IN WALNUT, EXECUTED BY KARL ROGENHOFER.
ARCHITECTS, KARL HOFMANN AND FELIX AUGENFELD, VIENNA

RESIDENCE IN VIENNA.   ARCHITECTS, F. KAYM AND A. HETMANEK, VIENNA
Materials: Furniture and beams of cherry wood: wall hangings of white tulle, green pile carpet—
white skin rug in bedroom

RESIDENCE IN MISTEK.   ARCHITECTS, F. KAYM AND A. HETMANEK, VIENNA
Materials: Woodwork in cherry wood and white tulle wall hangings

BATHROOM AND INTERIOR DESIGNED BY PIERRE CHAREAU, PARIS

STUDY DESIGNED AND EXECUTED BY PIERRE CHAREAU, PARIS.   TAPESTRY DESIGNED BY JEAN LURÇAT

COUNTRY HOUSE ON A BAVARIAN LAKE—SITTING-ROOM.   ARCHITECT, PROF. ERNST HAIGER.

SMOKING-ROOM OF A HOUSE IN BERLIN.   DESIGNED BY PROF. RICHARD RIEMERSCHMID, PASSING, NEAR MUNICH

TIMBER-BUILT HOLIDAY HOUSE AT AACHEN—THE SITTING-ROOM.   ARCHITECT, RICHARD RIEMERSCHMID,
PASSING, NEAR MUNICH

TIMBER-BUILT HOUSE, NEAR LEIPZIG—THE SMOKING-ROOM.   ARCHITECT, PROF. A. NIEMEYER, MUNICH

INTERIOR DESIGNED BY PROF. EMIL FAHRENKAMP, DÜSSELDORF
Furniture of mahogany; walls, rose and silver; hangings, grey and blue.

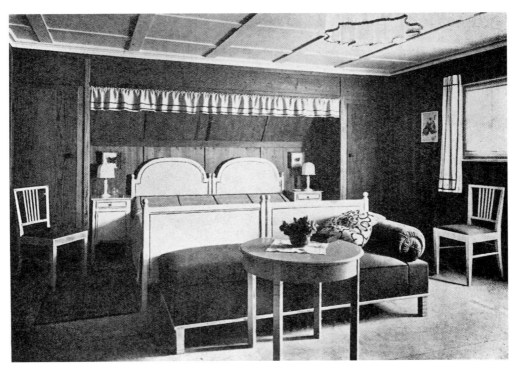

BEDROOM IN TIMBER-BUILT HOUSE, NEAR LEIPZIG. ARCHITECT, PROF. A. NIEMEYER, MUNICH

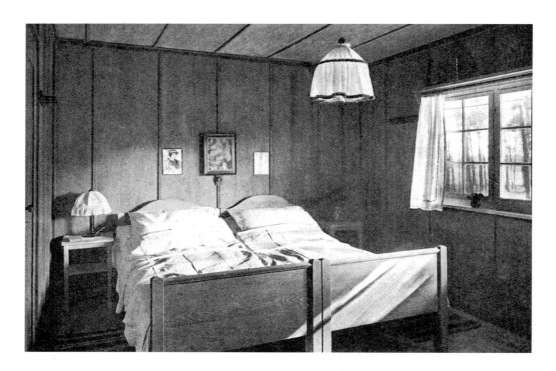

TIMBER-BUILT HOUSE AT HELLERAU, DRESDEN—BEDROOM AND SITTING-ROOM.   ARCHITECT, KARL BERTSCH, MUNICH

INTERIORS DESIGNED BY C. MALMSTEN, STOCKHOLM

HOUSE AT HIGHGATE.   ARCHITECT, C. H. B. QUENNELL, F.R.I.B.A., 43, BEDFORD ROW, LONDON

COTTAGE AT LEATHERHEAD.   ARCHITECTS, DARCY BRADDELL, F.R.I.B.A., AND HUMPHRY DEANE, 13, OLD
QUEBEC STREET, LONDON

BURFORD PRIORY, OXON—NORTH COURT AND
WEST WING. ARCHITECTS, WRATTEN, A.R.I.B.A.,
& GODFREY, 18, QUEEN ANNE'S GATE, LONDON

DESIGN FOR A DINING - ROOM
IN A SMALL COUNTRY HOUSE

HOUSE AT OXHEY. FROM A COLOURED DRAWING BY THE ARCHITECT, CYRIL A. FAREY, A.R.I.B.A., 19, BEDFORD SQUARE, LONDON

HOUSE DESIGNED BY A. D. THACKER, ARCHITECT, MONTREAL, CANADA
Rubble and frame building

HOUSES AT WILMERSDORF, BERLIN.   ARCHITECT, OTTO RUDOLF SALVISBERG, BERLIN, GERMANY
Materials : Walls, rough cast ; red roof ; shutters ultramarine

HOUSE IN MUNICH—THE GARDEN FRONT.   ARCHITECT, MAX WIEDERANDERS, MUNICH, GERMANY
Walls, blue-green   roof, dark red ; tiles, violet red

HOUSE AT DAHLEM—THE GATEWAY.   ARCHITECT, OTTO RUDOLF SALVISBERG, BERLIN, GERMANY

HOUSE AT MORGAT, FINISTÈRE, ARCHITECT. G. C. CHABAL, BREST, FRANCE

HOUSE AT MORGAT, FINISTÈRE.   ARCHITECT, G. C. CHABAL, BREST, FRANCE

HOUSE AT HIETZING.   ARCHITECT, PROF. JOSEF HOFFMANN,
VIENNA, AUSTRIA

HOUSE AT FREUDENTHAL—GARDEN FRONT.   ARCHITECT, PROF. JOSEF HOFFMANN, VIENNA, AUSTRIA

HOUSES AT LOUNY (CZECHOSLOVAKIA). ARCHITECT, JAN KOTĚRA, PRAGUE

WOODEN HOUSES AT THE AERODROME, PRAGUE, CZECHOSLOVAKIA. ARCHITECT, JOSEF GOČÁR, PRAGUE

RESIDENCE OF THE ARCHITECT, JENS
MOELLER JENSEN, GENTOFTE, DENMARK

COUNTRY HOUSE AT WASSENAAR, HOLLAND—TERRACE SIDE. RESIDENCE
OF THE ARCHITECT, A. J. KROPHOLLER, B.N.A.
Materials : Thatched roof ; orange Belgian bricks

" DE LUTTE," OLDENZAAL, HOLLAND. ARCHITECT, FOEKE KUIPERS, B.N.A., NAARDEN, HOLLAND

HOUSE AT STRANDGAARD.   ARCHITECTS, ARNOLD JENSEN AND NORBERG
Date and lintel above door designed and executed by Erling Höjgaard

" DE KEIZER," BOEKELO, HOLLAND.   ARCHITECT, FOEKE KUIPERS, B.N.A., NAARDEN

HOUSE NEAR BIRMINGHAM—THE HALL. ARCHITECTS, HARVEY AND
WICKS, BIRMINGHAM.

INTERIOR DESIGNED BY A. J. ROWLEY, 140, CHURCH STREET, KENSINGTON, LONDON
Rowlian silver gilt walls and inlaid wood panels

ROOM AT BROADWAY, WORCESTERSHIRE, AND DINING ROOM AT WARDLE, NEAR ROCHDALE. DESIGNED BY
S. GORDON RUSSELL AND EXECUTED BY RUSSELL AND SONS, BROADWAY, WORCS.

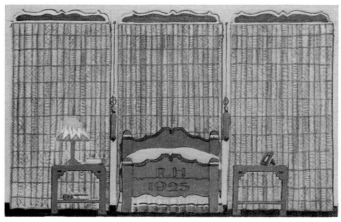

DESIGN FOR A SMALL BEDROOM
IN A HOUSE IN ESSEX, BY " S.L."

MOCKBEGGAR HILL, RINGWOOD, HAMPSHIRE.
—THE STUDY FROM THE SITTING - ROOM.
MURAL DECORATIONS AND HAND-PAINTED
CUSHION BY MAXWELL ARMFIELD, FROM
A DRAWING BY THE DESIGNER

BEDROOM DESIGNED BY "DIM," PARIS

HOUSE AT POCHMÜHL, AUSTRIA—LADY'S BED-
ROOM. ARCHITECT, PROF. JOSEF HOFFMANN,
VIENNA

DINING ROOM DESIGNED AND DECORATED BY "DOMINIQUE," PARIS
Wall faced with marble and stone pilastres ; silver handles to glass doors ; wrot iron radiator screens

DINING ROOM DESIGNED BY M. GUILLEMARD OF THE " ATELIER PRIMAVERA," PARIS

BEDROOM DESIGNED BY LOUIS SOGNOT OF THE " ATELIER PRIMAVERA," PARIS

HOUSE AT DAHLEM—THE HALL.   ARCHITECT, OTTO RUDOLF SALVISBERG, BERLIN

MUSIC ROOM.   ARCHITECT, PROFESSOR ERNST HAIGER, MUNICH, GERMANY
Walls cream ; Aubusson carpet ; gilt furniture ; Cobalt-blue taffeta upholstery

HOUSE AT HALENSEE, BERLIN. BOUDOIR IN STRAWBERRY AND RUSSET COLOURING RELIEVED WITH BLUE AND SILVER. DESIGNED BY OTTO FIRLE, DIPL. ENGINEER AND ARCHITECT, BERLIN, GERMANY

STUDY IN A TIMBER HOUSE DESIGNED BY PROFESSOR ALBINMÜLLER, ARCHITECT, DARMSTADT, GERMANY. EXECUTED BY CHRISTOPH AND UNMACK, A. G. NIESKY, O.L.

OAK STAIRCASE. DESIGNED AND EXECUTED BY MAX WIEDERANDERS, MUNICH, GERMANY

BACHELOR'S BEDROOM.   DESIGNED BY JACQUES RUHLMANN, PARIS

DRAWING ROOM BY MARCEL CHARPENTIER, PARIS
Mantelpiece of tiles ; furniture in ash

TWO FIREPLACES IN HOUSES AT ROTTERDAM.   ARCHITECT, N. P. DE KOO, ROTTERDAM, HOLLAND
(*Left*) *in hand worked stone*

STUDY WITH OAK WOODWORK.   DESIGNED BY PAUL BROMBERG, AMSTERDAM, AND EXECUTED BY
H. PANDER AND SONS, THE HAGUE, HOLLAND

TIMBERED HOUSE AT DRESDEN. ARCHITECT, PROFESSOR ADALBERT NIEMEYER, MUNICH. ERECTED BY THE DEUTSCHE WERKSTÄTTEN, A.G., MUNICH, GERMANY.

HOUSE AT DRESDEN. ARCHITECT, PROFESSOR BRUNO PAUL, BERLIN. ERECTED BY THE DEUTSCHE WERKSTÄTTEN, A.G., MUNICH, GERMANY.

COTTAGE FERRIBY
EAST YORKSHIRE
FOR H·ROUNTHWAITE ESQ

F.J.HORTH ARIBA
H·ANDREW ARIBA HULL

"COTTAGE FERRIBY," EAST YORK-
SHIRE. ARCHITECTS, HORTH AND
ANDREW, AA.R.I.B.A., HULL. FROM
A WATER-COLOUR BY F. J. HORTH

HOUSE AT STUTTGART—NORTH FRONT ELEVATION, MAIN ENTRANCE AND TRADESMAN'S
ENTRANCE. ARCHITECT, RUDOLF BEHR, STUTTGART, GERMANY

HOUSE AT STUTTGART—FRONT
ELEVATION, ARCHITECT, PRO-
FESSOR PAUL SCHMITTHENNER,
STUTTGART, GERMANY

"THE RIDGEWAY," CUFFLEY, HERTFORDSHIRE.
FROM A WATER-COLOUR BY THE ARCHITECT,
HUBERT LIDBETTER, A.R.I.B.A., AMBERLEY HOUSE,
NORFOLK STREET, STRAND, LONDON

"HEATHFIELD," HENLEY-ON-THAMES. ARCHITECTS, C. B. WILLCOCKS, F.R.I.B.A., AND J. R. GREENAWAY, F.S.I., READING

"MONKS WAY," SOUTHCOTE LANE, READING. ARCHITECTS, C. B. WILLCOCKS, F.R.I.B.A., AND J. R. GREENAWAY, F.S.I., READING

HOUSE ON THE RIVIERA—HALL AND STAIRCASE. ARCHITECT MARCEL DALMAS, NICE, FRANCE

SIDEBOARD IN SATINWOOD BY LOUIS SOGNOT;
DECORATIVE PANEL BY OLESIÉVISCZ;

NURSERY FURNITURE BY GUILLEMARD; DECOR-
ATIVE PANEL BY MLLE. CLAIRE FARGUE;

PRODUCED BY THE ATELIER PRIMAVERA, PARIS

STUDY FURNITURE IN EBONY
MACASSAR AND IVORY. DESIGNED
AND EXECUTED BY JACQUES RUHL-
MANN, PARIS

OCCASIONAL CHAIRS. DESIGNED BY EMANUEL
JOSEF MARGOLD, ARCHITECT, DARMSTADT, AND
EXECUTED BY H. BAHLSEN, BERLIN, GERMANY

WALNUT CABINET AND RED JAPANESE LACQUERED
CHAIR DESIGNED BY JULIUS BALLIN, ARCHITECT,
ERFURT, AND EXECUTED BY THE LUDWIGSBURGER
WERKSTÄTTEN. BATIK PANEL DESIGNED AND
EXECUTED BY ERICA BALLIN-WOLTERICK

LIVING ROOM DESIGNED BY K. BERTSCH, AND EXECUTED BY THE DEUTSCHE
WERKSTÄTTEN, A.G., MUNICH, GERMANY

DESIGN FOR A MUSIC ROOM BY
GEORGE SHERINGHAM, BESANT
COTTAGE, FROGNAL, LONDON

BUNGALOW AT BIRCHALL, LEEK.   ARCHITECTS, R. T. LONGDEN, F.R.I.B.A., AND W. J. VENABLES, L.R.I.B.A., LEEK

HOUSE AT BIRCHALL, LEEK.   ARCHITECTS, R. T. LONGDEN, F.R.I.B.A., AND W. J. VENABLES, L.R.I.B.A., LEEK

COUNTRY HOUSE IN LENNEP—THE TERRACE.   ARCHITECT, F. W. HOEFFKEN, LENNEP, RHINELAND, GERMANY

HOUSE IN GRUNEWALD-BERLIN.   ARCHITECT, OSKAR KAUFMANN, BERLIN, GERMANY

BEDROOM FURNITURE IN OLD ROSE JAPANESE LACQUER.   DESIGNED BY JULIUS BALLIN. ARCHITECT,
ERFURT, AND EXECUTED BY THE LUDWIGSBURGER WERKSTÄTTEN, GERMANY

STUDY DESIGNED BY PROFESSOR E. FAHRENKAMP, ARCHITECT, DÜSSELDORF, GERMANY

HOUSE AT DRESDEN—THE STUDY.
DESIGNED BY PROFESSOR BRUNO
PAUL, ARCHITECT, BERLIN, AND
EXECUTED BY THE DEUTSCHE
WERKSTÄTTEN, A.G., MUNICH,
GERMANY.

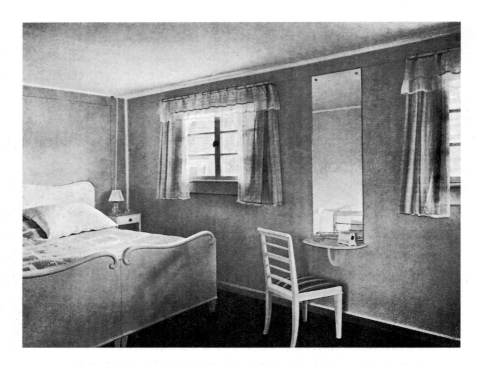

HOUSE AT DRESDEN—BEDROOM AND SIDEBOARD. DESIGNED BY PROFESSOR BRUNO PAUL, ARCHITECT, BERLIN, AND EXECUTED BY THE DEUTSCHE WERKSTÄTTEN, A.G., MUNICH, GERMANY

FIREPLACE AND ARMCHAIR
DESIGNED AND EXECUTED
BY "DOMINIQUE," PARIS

HALL FIREPLACE. DESIGNED BY PROFESSOR O. O.
KURZ, ARCHITECT, MUNICH, GERMANY. FIGURE BY
PROFESSOR ERWIN KURZ, SCULPTOR.

STUDIO IN MANNHEIM. TERRA-COTTA FIRE-PLACE
IN RED ROOM. DESIGNED BY EMANUEL JOSEF
MARGOLD, ARCHITECT, DARMSTADT, GERMANY

FIREPLACE IN STUDY. DESIGNED BY PROFESSOR E. FAHRENKAMP, ARCHITECT, DÜSSELDORF,
GERMANY

DINING ROOM WITH PANELLING
OF PLYWOOD SHEETS FIXED
DIRECT TO WALLS WITH MOULDED
RAILS, ETC. DOOR MADE OF IBUS
BOARD, PAINTED

FIREPLACE IN HOUSE AT BEVERWIJK, AND INTERIOR OF COUNTRY HOUSE AT ZANDVOORT. ARCHITECT, A. J. KROPHOLLER, WASSENAAR, HOLLAND

SITTING ROOM. DESIGNED BY PAUL BROMBERG, AND EXECUTED BY H. PANDER AND SONS, THE HAGUE, HOLLAND

HOUSE IN BERLIN—FIREPLACE
DESIGNED BY OSKAR KAUFMANN,
ARCHITECT, BERLIN.

A PARTIAL VIEW OF AN IMPORTANT
READING ROOM BY E. J. RUHLMANN,
DECORATOR, 27 RUE DE LISBONNE,
PARIS

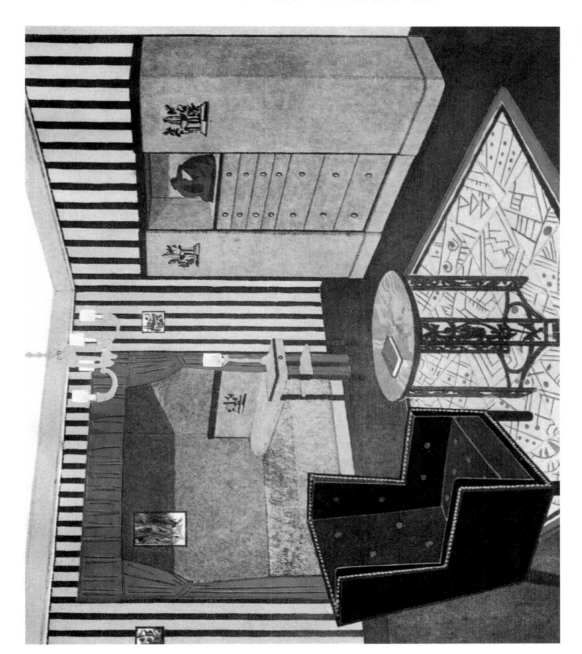

YOUNG MAN'S BEDROOM DESIGNED BY
M. GUILLEMARD. PRODUCED BY ATELIER
PRIMAVERA

"FIELD PLACE," WILLINGDON, SUSSEX.   ARCHITECT, JOHN D. CLARKE, F.R.I.B.A., EASTBOURNE

*The windows in this house are of particular interest; they slide down out of sight
into a cavity in the wall*

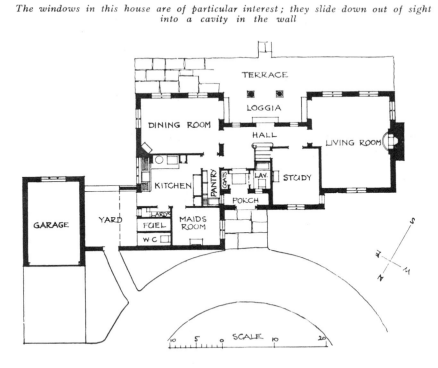

FIELD PLACE," WILLINGDON,
SUSSEX — DETAIL OF LOGGIA.
ARCHITECT, JOHN D. CLARKE,
F.R.I.B.A., EASTBOURNE

PORTMEIRION—A MODEL OF THE VILLAGE
ON THE CAMBRIAN COAST. ARCHITECT,
CLOUGH WILLIAMS-ELLIS, 22B, EBURY
STREET, LONDON.

PORTMEIRION, NORTH WALES.
Another view

PORTMEIRION NORTH WALES.
ARCHITECT, CLOUGH WILLIAMS-ELLIS,
228, EBURY STREET, LONDON

HOUSE AT PORTMEIRION, NORTH WALES.   ARCHITECT, CLOUGH WILLIAMS-ELLIS, 22^b, EBURY
STREET, LONDON.   (*Below*) DETAIL OF ENTRANCE PORCH.
An attempt has been made in this new Cambrian coast village to arrive at a blend of Welsh
traditional building and that of Northern Italy which will harmonise with, and even enhance
the curiously Italianate nature of the site.

GROUND FLOOR

No. 33, STOREY'S WAY, CAM-
BRIDGE — PART OF ENTRANCE
FRONT. ARCHITECTS, BAILLIE
SCOTT AND BERESFORD, 8,
GRAY'S INN SQUARE, LONDON

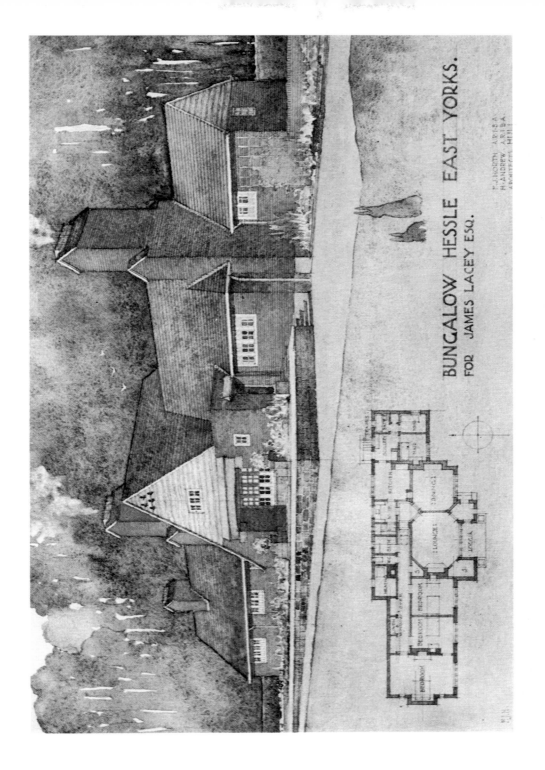

BUNGALOW HESSLE EAST YORKS.

FOR JAMES LACEY ESQ.

BUNGALOW AT HESSLE. ARCHITECTS,
F. J. HORTH, A.R.I.B.A., AND H. ANDREW,
A.R.I.B.A., HULL. FROM A DRAWING
BY F. J. HORTH

HOUSE AT GROSSE POINTE, MICHIGAN. VIEW FROM GARDEN. ARCHITECT, A. HOPKINS, NEW YORK

HOUSE AT HORNBECH, DENMARK. ARCHITECT, HANNING HANSEN

"NEW WAYS," NORTHAMPTON,
RESIDENCE OF W. J. BASSETT-
LOWKE, ESQ. ENTRANCE DOOR-
WAY AND STAIRCASE WINDOW.
ARCHITECT, PROFESSOR DR. P.
BEHRENS, VIENNA.

TWO SCHEMES FOR INTERIOR DECORA-
TION BY THE ROWLEY GALLERY, 140,
CHURCH STREET, KENSINGTON, FROM
DRAWINGS BY HENRY BUTLER

MURAL DECORATION IN A DINING-ROOM AT 21, BEDFORD STREET, LIVERPOOL, RESIDENCE OF PROF. C. H. REILLY. DESIGNED AND EXECUTED BY MARY ADSHEAD, SUNBURY-ON-THAMES

" NEW WAYS," NORTHAMPTON—THE LOUNGE, ARCHITECT, PROFESSOR DR. P. BEHRENS, VIENNA. FIREPLACE BY THE ALLIED ARTS AND CRAFTS GUILD, BIRMINGHAM

HOUSE AT RADLETT HERTS. A BRICK CHIMNEY-PIECE. ARCHITECTS : M. E. WALKER, F.R.I.B.A., AND A. W. HARWOOD, A.R.I.B.A., 21, SUFFOLK STREET, PALL MALL EAST, LONDON

" RANMORE," WEST BYFLEET—THE DINING-ROOM FIREPLACE. ARCHITECT GERALD WARREN, F.R.I.B.A., 12, NORFOLK STREET, STRAND, LONDON.

"NEW WAYS," NORTHAMPTON—RESIDENCE OF W. J. BASSETT-LOWKE, ESQ.   ARCHITECT, PROFESSOR
DR. P. BEHRENS, VIENNA.   THE HALL SHOWING PISCINA AND BUILT-IN CLOCK.

*Walls of primrose distemper. Wood work matt grey enamel. Furniture and stair-
case cappings of black wood. Tiles black, grey and white. Stair carpet royal blue.*

A BEDROOM AT "FIELD PLACE," WILLING-
DON, SUSSEX. ARCHITECT, JOHN D.
CLARKE, F.R.I.B.A., EASTBOURNE.

A BEDROOM AT STRAFFORD LODGE,
WEYBRIDGE. DESIGNED BY JOSEPH EMBER-
TON, A.R.I.B.A.

STRAFFORD LODGE, WEYBRIDGE—BEDROOM. DESIGNED BY JOSEPH EMBERTON, A.R.I.B.A.,
150, REGENT STREET, LONDON.
Twin beds in unstained sycamore inlaid with walnut finished with dull polish

STRAFFORD LODGE, WEYBRIDGE, RESI-
DENCE OF L. H. SECCOMBE, ESQ. BEDROOM
DESIGNED BY JOSEPH EMBERTON,
A.R.I.B.A., 150, REGENT STREET, LONDON.
*Walls of a beige colour
with gold decoration, cream ceiling, carpet skirtings
and woodwork in French grey*

CORNER OF A SITTING-ROOM
IN LARCH, DESIGNED BY HANS
DÖLLGAST.   EXECUTED   BY
RUDOLF LORENZ, VIENNA

BEDROOM IN A COUNTRY COTTAGE. DESIGNED BY FRANZ KAYM AND ALFONS HETMANEK,
ARCHITECTS, VIENNA

LIVING ROOM IN A COUNTRY COTTAGE. DESIGNED BY FRANZ KAYM AND ALFONS HETMANEK,
ARCHITECTS, VIENNA

INTERIOR DESIGNED BY PIERRE CHAREAU, PARIS. BAS-RELIEF BY JACQUES LIPCHITZ
White walls rough-cast; grey carpet; jade green curtains; smoke-colour
upholstery

DRAWING-ROOM DESIGNED BY L. SOGNOT (ATELIER PRIMAVERA) PRODUCED BY MAGASINS
DU PRINTEMPS, PARIS

BEDROOM DESIGNED BY MARCEL GUILLEMARD, CARPET BY THOMAS (ATELIER PRIMAVERA)
PRODUCED BY MAGASINS DU PRINTEMPS, PARIS

INTERIOR BY LORD AND TAYLOR, NEW YORK CITY
*Small Furniture in Modernist Style, painted yellow, green and red. Doors are
yellow, painted in red, green and violet design*

ALCOVE IN PINE KITCHEN AT BEAUPORT, GLOUCESTER, MASSACHUSSETTS. EARLY
AMERICAN FURNITURE
*The woodwork and many details were from the Barker " garrison " house at
Pembroke, Massachussetts. Colour, natural old red pine*

CORNER OF A SITTING-ROOM.
DESIGNED BY K. HOFMANN AND F.
AUGENFELD, EXECUTED BY KARL
SCHREITL, VIENNA. *Panels of walnut
with door-frame of veined alder.*

SMALL HOUSE AT FINCHLEY. ARCHITECT, P. D. HEPWORTH, F.R.I.B.A., 7, GRAY'S INN PLACE, LONDON. FROM A DRAWING BY THE ARCHITECT

BEDROOM IN PARIS DESIGNED
BY JOUBERT ET PETIT, PRO-
DUCED BY "D.I.M." (*from "In-
térieurs," Léon Moussinac, Editions
Albert Lévy, Paris*)

DINING-ROOM DESIGNED AND EXECUTED BY FRANCIS JOURDAIN, PARIS

DINING-ROOM DESIGNED BY MARCEL GUILLEMARD (ATELIER PRIMAVERA)
PRODUCED BY MAGASINS DU PRINTEMPS, PARIS

DINING-ROOM IN A HOUSE IN
BOULOGNE - SUR - SEINE. DE-
SIGNED BY LUCIE RENAUDOT.
EXECUTED BY A. DUMAS

SMALL BOUDOIR IN WILD CHERRY AND ASH; BLUE AND SILVER DAMASK ON THE WALLS. DESIGNED BY "DOMINIQUE" PARIS

VILLA AT LA NARTELLE—THE HALL DECORATED WITH MOSAICS AND ENAMEL. ARCHITECT, L. BAILLY. SCULPTURE BY DILIGENT, WINDOW BY JACQUES GRUBER

GIRL'S BEDROOM IN PARIS, DESIGNED AND
EXECUTED BY NATHAN, PARIS

BATHROOM IN PIASTRIACCIA MARBLE, DESIGNED AND EXECUTED BY JACQUES RUHLMANN, PARIS

ROOM IN A FLAT IN THE AVENUE CHAMPS ELYSÉES, PARIS.   DESIGNED BY JACQUES RUHLMANN.   CARVED PANEL BY RIGAL
Chairs upholstered in Aubusson tapestry.   Panelling of polished ebony;
furniture in macassar ebony

CIRCULAR STUDY. DESIGNED AND
EXECUTED BY JACQUES RUHLMANN,
PARIS. *Panelling painted green with
gilded moulding ; furniture in macassar ebony*

HOUSES AT BREMEN, GERMANY.   ARCHITECTS, RUNGE AND
SCOTLAND, BREMEN

HOUSES ON THE SCHWACHHAUSER RING, BREMEN, GERMANY.   ARCHITECTS, RUNGE AND SCOTLAND,
BREMEN

DESIGN FOR A HALL BY
HANS HARTL, ARCHITECT,
ESSEN, GERMANY

HOUSES IN "THE ORCHARD," WELWYN GARDEN CITY. ARCHITECTS, LOUIS DE SOISSONS, F.R.I.B.A., AND
ARTHUR W. KENYON, F.R.I.B.A., OFFICE OF WELWYN GARDEN CITY, LTD. BUILDERS, WELWYN BUILDERS, LTD.

HOUSES IN GUESSENS ROAD, WELWYN GARDEN CITY. ARCHITECTS, LOUIS DE SOISSONS, F.R.I.B.A., AND ARTHUR W. KENYON, F.R.I.B.A., OFFICE OF WELWYN GARDEN CITY, LTD. BUILDERS, ADAMS & SON, WELWYN.

GENERAL VIEW OF HOUSES IN GUESSENS ROAD, WELWYN GARDEN CITY.

HOUSE AT CROMER, NORFOLK.   ARCHITECTS, A. F. SCOTT AND SONS, F.F.R.I.B.A., 23, TOMBLAND, NORWICH

HOUSE AT CROMER, NORFOLK.   ARCHITECTS, A. F. SCOTT AND SONS, F.F.R.I.B.A., 23, TOMBLAND, NORWICH.   BUILDERS OF BOTH HOUSES, CHILDS AND SPINKS, CROMER.

PAIR OF HOUSES, BURY STREET, RUISLIP. ARCHITECT, ARCH. S. SOUTAR, 8, KING WILLIAM STREET, STRAND, LONDON. BUILDER, C. W. MYHILL, RUISLIP.

PAIR OF HOUSES ON CORNER SITE AT RUISLIP. ARCHITECT, ARCH. S. SOUTAR, 8, KING WILLIAM STREET, STRAND, LONDON. BUILDER, C. W. MYHILL, RUISLIP.

ROW OF SIX-ROOM HOUSES, SUNNYSIDE GARDENS, LONG ISLAND, NEW YORK.   ARCHITECTS, CLARENCE S. STEIN.   ASSOCIATE, HENRY WRIGHT

HOUSES FOR ONE, TWO AND THREE FAMILIES, SUNNYSIDE GARDENS, LONG ISLAND, NEW YORK.   ARCHITECTS, CLARENCE S. STEIN.   ASSOCIATE, HENRY WRIGHT

MODEL HOUSES IN MARIEMONT, THE NEW VILLAGE, ADJOINING CINCINNATI, OHIO.   PART OF FIFTY HOMES, IN
"GROUP HOUSING" PLAN, DESIGNED BY RICHARD H. DANA, JNR.

*The cost of these houses makes them available to skilled manual workers and clerks.   Mr. Dana, with Mr. C. J.
Livingood (President of the Mariemont Company), bought all the furnishings for 500 dollars, at retail, to show how
reasonably such a home can be fitted out.*

HOUSES IN ORLEANSSTRASSE, BREMEN, GERMANY.   ARCHITECTS, RUNGE AND SCOTLAND, BREMEN

DINING ROOM IN ALUMINIUM AND "DUCO." DESIGNED BY DJO-BOURGEOIS, PARIS. CARPETS AND CURTAINS BY ELISE DJO-BOURGEOIS.

BEDROOM WITH FURNITURE IN SYCAMORE. DESIGNED BY MARCEL GUILLEMARD (ATELIER PRIMAVERA), PARIS

CORNER OF A DINING ROOM
DESIGNED BY KARL PULLICH,
WIESBADEN: EXECUTED BY
J G. MÖRGENTHALER, ZUFFEN-
HAUSEN, GERMANY

DINING ROOM IN THE HOUSE OF MONSIEUR SCHWOB, PARIS.   DESIGNED BY DJO-BOURGEOIS, PARIS

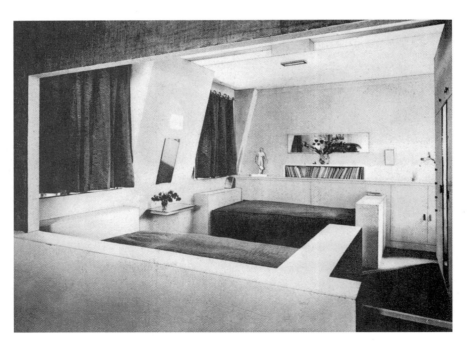

BEDROOM DESIGNED FOR A YACHT BY DJO-BOURGEOIS, PARIS.   CARPET BY ELISE DJO-BOURGEOIS

CORNER OF A BOUDOIR DESIGNED BY RENÉ
PROU. WALLS LINED WITH VARNISHED
SYCAMORE. CHIMNEY PIECE IN WHITE
MARBLE

TWO VIEWS OF A BEDROOM DESIGNED BY A. FRECHET: PRODUCED BY E. VÉROT, PARIS
*Furniture in varnished sycamore : walls hung with pale grey moiré ;
counterpane of fur edged with violet taffeta and head curtain of the same.*

INTERIOR DESIGNED BY P. GENET AND L. MICHON, PARIS. WALLS AND CHANDELIER OF PRESSED GLASS

CORNER OF A BED SITTING ROOM. DESIGNED BY PIERRE CHAREAU, PARIS
Painted in grey, ivory and écru : interior of shelves coral.

RECEPTION OFFICE DESIGNED
BY MONTAGNAC, PARIS. BRONZE
FIGURE BY LOUIS DEJEAN

TWO ASPECTS OF A HOUSE
NEAR FRANKFURT - AM - MAIN.
ARCHITECT, HUGO EBERHARDT,
OFFENBACH-AM-MAIN, GERMANY

HOUSE AT HEIDELBERG.   ARCHITECT, MARTIN ELSAESSER, FRANKFURT-AM-MAIN, GERMANY

HOUSE OF THE ARCHITECT, MARTIN ELSAESSER, AT FRANKFURT-AM-MAIN, GERMANY

Mrs. WHITLOW'S HOUSE at HAMPSTEAD

F E GREEN delt

HOUSE AT HAMPSTEAD,
ARCHITECT, HUBERT
LIDBETTER, A.R.I.B.A.,
12, NORFOLK STREET,
STRAND, LONDON

A DINING ROOM DESIGNED BY AUGUST TRUEB, ARCHITECT, STUTTGART, GERMANY. *Reproduced by courtesy of Walter Hädecke Verlag, Stuttgart, from " Räume und Menschen "*

BEDROOM AND LIVING ROOM IN A COTTAGE AT BROADWAY.   ARCHITECT, LESLIE MANSFIELD, F.R.I.B.A.:
FURNITURE DESIGNED BY GORDON RUSSELL, THE RUSSELL WORKSHOPS, LTD., BROADWAY, WORCS.

COTTAGE AT BROADWAY. ARCHITECT, LESLIE MANSFIELD, F.R.I.B.A. FURNITURE DESIGNED BY GORDON RUSSELL, THE RUSSELL WORKSHOPS, LTD., BROADWAY, WORCS.

HOUSE AT DORSINGTON. PANELLING DESIGNED BY LESLIE MANSFIELD, F.R.I.B.A., AND GORDON RUSSELL. FURNITURE DESIGNED BY GORDON RUSSELL, THE RUSSELL WORKSHOPS, LTD., BROADWAY, WORCS.

CORNER OF A BOUDOIR, DESIGNED BY LOUIS SOGNOT (ATELIER PRIMAVERA), PARIS

BEDROOM IN SYCAMORE AND CITRON WOOD, DESIGNED BY E. KOHLMANN: PRODUCED BY STUDIUM LOUVRE, PARIS

PRIVATE BAR IN A FLAT, DESIGNED BY F. AND G. SADDIER:
PRODUCED BY SADDIER ET SES FILS, PARIS

PRIVATE BAR IN A PARIS FLAT, DESIGNED BY DJO-BOURGEOIS, PARIS: CARPET BY ELISE
DJO-BOURGEOIS

STUDIO IN MAHOGANY AND BUBENGA, DESIGNED BY JEAN AND JACQUES ADNET: PRODUCED
BY SADDIER ET SES FILS, PARIS

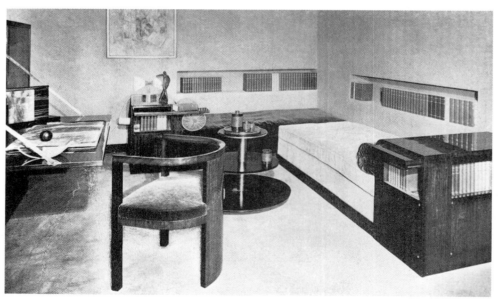

CORNER OF A STUDIO IN PEROBA WOOD, DESIGNED BY JEAN AND JACQUES ADNET: PRODUCED
BY SADDIER ET SES FILS, PARIS

DINING ROOM SUITE IN GREY
LACQUER DESIGNED BY MAURICE
MATET : PRODUCED BY STUDIUM
LOUVRE, PARIS

STUDIO DINING ROOM, DESIGNED AND PRODUCED BY PIERRE CHAREAU, PARIS
Walls, ceiling and bookcase yellow ; curtains of grey, white and yellow check ; armchair covered in silver and tête-de-nègre, mosaic pattern ; table in Cuban mahogany ; lamp of steel and alabaster

DINING ROOM IN VARNISHED WHITE SYCAMORE. ARCHITECT, G. E. J. J. DENNERY : ART DIRECTOR, LÉON BOUCHET, PARIS

CORNER OF A STUDIO, DESIGNED BY PIERRE CHAREAU, PARIS

Walls painted beige and three tones of grey: furniture in palisander, upholstered in pig-skin and "mosaic" material: curtains of grey, green and tête-de-nègre check: carpet in brown, yellow and beige (after a design by Papasoff)

(*Above*) *House in Hampshire. Architect,* GERALD UNSWORTH, *F.R.I.B.A.,* 8 *Conduit Street, London, W.*1. (*Below*) *House near Kenilworth. Architect, C. M. C.* ARMSTRONG, *F.R.I.B.A.,* 39 *High Street, Warwick.*

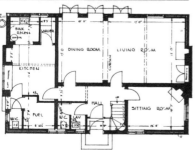

GROUND FLOOR PLAN

Two views of Beck Hall, Sutton, Sussex, showing alterations and additions. Architect, GERALD WARREN, F.R.I.B.A., Amberley House, Norfolk Street, London.

Ground Floor Plan

First Floor Plan

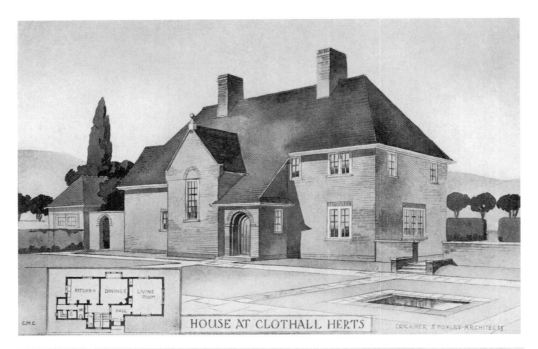

HOUSE AT CLOTHALL HERTS

(Above) House at Clothall, Herts. Architect, C. M. CRICKMER, F.R.I.B.A. and ALLEN FOXLEY, M.A., 1 Lincoln's Inn Fields, London, W.C.2. *(Below)* House at Headington, Oxon. Walls rough cast, wood and iron work painted white, Harts Hill tiles and chimney bricks. Architect, HERBERT L. NORTH, F.RI.B.A., Llanfairfechan, Caernarvonshire.

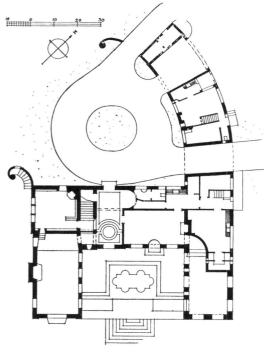

House at Hurtwood, Surrey (West elevation).
Architect, OLIVER HILL, F.R.I.B.A., 9 Hanover
Square, London, W.1.

(*Above*) *House built of concrete masonry and Portland Cement stucco for Mr. E. J. Longyear, Altadena, California. Architect,* WILLIAM LEE WOOLLETT, *Los Angeles.* (*Below*) *House of concrete masonry surfaced with Portland Cement stucco for Mr I. Eisner, Los Angeles. Left, the entrance : right, the loggia. Architect,* GORDON B. KAUFMANN.

House in Los Angeles, California, built of concrete masonry for Mr. I. Eisner.   Architect, GORDON B. KAUFMANN.

(Above, left) Nursery landing and staircase in the house of Dr. Kriebel : "wall" banister, with two handrails : walls covered with linoleum. Architect, ADOLF RADING, Berlin. (Above, right) Staircase designed by WALTER GROPIUS, Berlin.
(Below) Dining-room, leading on to terrace, in the house at Stuttgart-Weissenhof designed by HANS SCHAROUN, Berlin.

(Above) Brick and concrete house in the Avenue Seghers, Brussels. (Below) South aspect of house at Stuttgart-Weissenhof, Germany, constructed of hollow pumice slabs   *Architect,*
VICTOR BOURGEOIS, *Avenue Seghers,* 103, *Brussels.*

(Above) " Le Chateau," built for Mr. Crittall. Construction of brickwork, cement rendered, and washed ivory : window bars painted emerald green. (Below) House for Mr. Smith, constructed in brickwork, colour washed. The water storage tank is on the roof, over oriel window of front balcony. Entrance door painted rich blue, window bars emerald green. The windows are standard steel casements, with vertical glazing bars omitted. Both houses form part of Silver End Village. Architect, THOMAS S. TAIT, F.R.I.B.A. (Sir John Burnet and Partners), 1, Montagu Place, London, W.C.1.

House for Mr. Small, in Silver End Village, constructed in brickwork, washed cream colour. Entrance door painted rich orange, window bars emerald green. The water storage tank is on roof over oriel window of front balcony. The windows are standard steel casements with vertical glazing bars omitted. Architect, THOMAS S. TAIT, F.R.I.B.A. (Sir John Burnet and Partners), 1 Montagu Place, London, W.C.1.

(Above) Block of four parlour-type cottages, Silver End Village, constructed of brick, washed cream colour. *The windows are standard steel casements, painted green, with vertical glazing bars omitted. Architect, THOMAS S. TAIT (Sir John Burnet and Partners), London. (Below) House at Edgbaston, Birmingham, built of brick and concrete, and designed to minimise household labour, with entire absence of fireplaces, passages, dark corners and woodwork (except floors and doors). The rooms are planned to admit all available sunlight, and are heated by wall panels. There are sun porches on ground and first floors. In the kitchen, there are special fitments for easy preparation and serving of meals Architects, DOUGLAS G. TANNER and ARTHUR L HORSBURGH, Great Western Buildings, Livery Street, Birmingham.*

(Above) A great impression of air and space is achieved by this living-room designed by Adolf Rading. In the foreground are folding doors which can divide the room into two, and large windows open on to a terrace. (Below) A dining-room which can at will be made into an open air room by means of sliding windows is a charming feature of this house designed by Hans Scharoun. A built-in cupboard and two steps divide it from the living-room.

(Above) This bedroom designed by Richard Döcker has many interesting features.   The built-in bed has the addition of a side-table, and the circular dressing table has a stool which fits into the front aperture.   (Below) A charming bedroom with furniture designed by Richard Lisker has an interesting dressing-table with a horizontal light above it. A similar lamp is fixed over the bed-head.

Sitting-room designed by Jean-Michel Frank.

(*Above*) *House at Frankfurt-am-Main-Ginnheim, Germany* (*South aspect*), *built of brick, faced with plaster.*
(*Below*) *Interior of living-room in the architect's house at Frankfurt-am-Main. Architect,* ERNST MAY, *Germany.*

Garden entrance of the architect's house at Frankfurt-am-Main. Construction of brickwork, faced with concrete. *Architect, ERNST MAY, Frankfurt-am-Main, Germany.*

Small week-end house, built of timber, showing studio in tower.   Architect, HARRY ROSENTHAL, Berlin.

Villa at Garches, near Paris (North elevation). Architects, LE CORBUSIER AND P. JEANNERET, *Rue de Sèvres,* 35, *Paris. The construction consists of reinforced concrete members, spaced out at regular intervals. There is therefore no restriction to the size of the windows, which run continuously across the elevation, as shown in the illustration. The floor areas are entirely free, and can be divided up with partitions without restriction. The roof is flat and utilised as a garden: this provides the most efficacious means of counteracting expansion in the concrete*

Villa at Garches, near Paris. (Above) North elevation : (below) the roof garden. Architects, LE CORBUSIER and P. JEANNERET, Rue de Sèvres, 35, Paris.

Villa at Garches, near Paris.   (Above) The roof garden: (below) South aspect.   Architects, LE CORBUSIER and P. JEANNERET, Rue de Sèvres, 35, Paris.

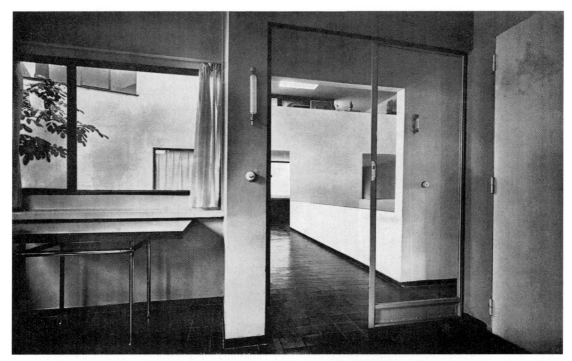

(Above) Interior of reinforced concrete house at Auteuil, France. Architects, LE CORBUSIER and P. JEANNERET, Rue de Sèvres, 35, Paris. (Below) The Casino at Saint-Jean-de-Luz, built of reinforced concrete. Architect, ROB MALLET-STEVENS, Rue Mallet-Stevens, Paris. The flooring is of inlaid " Noel " mahogany : walls painted white, with strips of wood painted lemon colour and black : furniture of nickelled steel, upholstered in lemon and black linen : casements and electric light fittings of metal.

House of Monsieur and Madame Bressy, 27, Villa Saïd, Paris (the entrance hall). Architects, A. and G. PERRET, Paris. The columns of reinforced concrete support the weight of the whole house : both walls and columns are covered with seamless stucco : doors of fumed oak : staircase of stone, with forged iron banister.

(*Above*) House of Madame Froriep de Salis at Boulogne-sur-Seine. Architect, ANDRÉ LURCAT, Paris. The flat roof is used as a garden : pavement tiles and flower-bed borders in concrete.

(*Below*) House of Monsieur and Madame Bressy, 27, Villa Said, Paris. Architects, A. and G. PERRET, Paris. The skeleton of this house is of reinforced concrete, the external angles of the elevation being in hard stone.

House of Madame Froriep de Salis at Boulogne-sur-Seine.   Architect, ANDRE LURCAT, Paris.   The construction consists of reinforced concrete posts and beams, the spaces left being filled with hollow bricks, and the whole wall then faced with cement or stone.

(*Above*) Interior of the house of Monsieur and Madame Bressy, 27, Villa Saïd, Paris, showing the stone staircase, with forged iron banister. The walls are lined with stucco, and the window framework is in reinforced concrete. Architects, A. and G. PERRET, Paris. (*Below*) Flats at Bagneux, France, showing the garden entrance, constructed in reinforced concrete, with windows and doors painted cobalt blue. Architect, ANDRE LURCAT, Paris.

Block of flats at Bagneux, France, constructed in reinforced concrete (view from the street). The doors and windows are painted cobalt blue. Architect, ANDRE LURCAT, Paris.

(above) KARL HOFMANN & FELIX AUGENFELD, Architects, Vienna. Bedroom suite in Corborella wood. Executed by V. Kabele. (below) FRITZ GROSS, Architect, Vienna. Dining table and glass cupboard in Caucasian walnut. Executed by Carl Hamberger.

FRITZ GROSS, Architect, Vienna. Combined living-room, study and bedroom. Stove of masonry, brick and ceramic, executed by Fessler.

(Above) House at Stuttgart-Weissenhof, Germany, constructed by semi-dry building process on concrete foundations : walls of hollow blocks of pumice (" Moskopf " system), faced with plaster : inner surface of walls covered with composition boards : roof insulated with cork lining. (Reproduced from " Bau and Wohnung " by courtesy of Akademischer Verlag Dr. Fritz Wedekind and Co., Stuttgart). (Below) Semi-detached house at Dessau, Germany, built of " Jurko " slag concrete. The flat roofs are all accessible for use. Architect of both houses, WALTER GROPIUS, Potsdamerstrasse, 121a, Berlin, W.35.

(Above) Small house at Dessau, Germany, built of " Jurko " slag concrete, with flat roof. (Below) House at Stuttgart-Weissenhof, Germany, constructed of dry concrete slabs on rolled steel framework, supported on platform, or raft, of reinforced concrete : walls faced externally with asbestos slabs, and internally with " Expansit " cork boards : interior walls and ceilings faced with " Celotex " boards. (Reproduced from " Bau and Wohnung " by courtesy of Akademischer Verlag Dr. Fritz Wedekind and Co., Stuttgart). Architect of both houses, WALTER GROPIUS, Potsdamerstrasse, 121a, Berlin, W.35.

(Above) House of Herr Berthold at Leipzig, constructed in brick, with Luxfer prism window panes : view from the garden. (Below) House of Herr Dahlewitz : interior and exterior view of the staircase window, constructed of Luxfer prism panes set in concrete. Architect of both houses, BRUNO TAUT, Potsdamerstrasse, 129-130, Berlin, W.9.

House of Herr Dahlewitz, constructed in brick. (Above) View from the garden. (Below) Interior of study, on the ground floor. Architect, BRUNO TAUT, Potsdamerstrasse, 129-130, Berlin, W.9.

Two houses at Stuttgart-Weissenhof, Germany, constructed of portable " Thermos " slabs mounted on steel frame
Architect, MAX TAUT, Potsdamerstrasse, 129-130, Berlin, W.9.

Two views of a living-room interior in a house at Stuttgart-Weissenhof, Germany.   Architect, MAX TAUT, Potsdamerstrasse, 129-130, Berlin, W.9.   Furniture designed by RICHARD HERRE, Stuttgart.

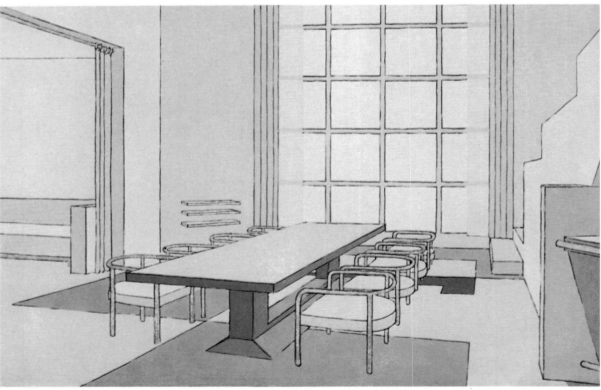

Two designs by DJO-BOURGEOIS, Paris. Above is a bedroom, with built-in fittings, including a desk in the corner, conveniently placed next the windows. The dining-room below is an attractive example of modern simplicity and convenience.

A small drawing-room designed by FRANCIS JOURDAIN, Paris, with walls, chairs and sofas covered with textiles by HELENE HENRY, and a lacquered table. Luminous panels of glass are set in the walls. The carpet is by MYRBOR.

House at Stuttgart-Weissenhof, Germany. (Above) Exterior view of the house, which is constructed of " Fonitram " slabs, for heat insulation, on timber framework. and coated with plaster. (Below) The garden room seen from the dining room, from which it is divided by glass partitions and doors. The living rooms, kitchen and bedrooms all face South on to the garden. (From " Bau und Wohnung," by courtesy of Akademischer Verlag Dr. Fritz Wedekind & Co., Stuttgart.) Architect, HANS POELZIG. Hardenbergstr., 33, Berlin-Charlottenberg.

House at Stuttgart-Weissenhof, Germany. (Above) The verandah, and (below) view from the garden.

Architect, HANS POELZIG, Hardenbergstr., 33, Berlin-Charlottenberg.

(Above) House at Liegnitz Garden City, Germany, constructed of wooden slabs (Christoph & Unmack's system) : exterior painted red, grey and white. (Below) View of the kitchen in model dwelling at Stuttgart-Weissenhof   *Architect, HANS SCHAROUN,*
Kronprinzen Ufer, 19/11, Berlin, N.W. 40.

Two views of a house at Stuttgart-Weissenhof, Germany. Construction of steel framework, faced with pumice slabs, inside and out, coloured white and grey: small surfaces yellow and red; walls and ceilings covered with Lincrusta in light grey, medium grey, light and dark blue, and black. Architect, HANS SCHAROUN, Kronprinzen Ufer, 19/11, Berlin, N.W. 40.

(*Above*) *One-storey house at Westendheim, Frankfurt-am-Main, Germany, constructed on Stadtbaurat May's ferro-concrete slab system.   Architect, ADOLF MEYER, Städtisches Hochbauamt, Frankfurt-am-Main.* (*Below*) *House at Stuttgart-Weissenhof, Germany, constructed of large hollow bricks : partition walls and ceilings of wood, " Feifel " system.*   *Architect, LUDWIG HILBERSEIMER, Einser Strasse, 14, Berlin-Wilmersdorf.*

House at Stuttgart-Weissenhof, Germany. (Above) View from the street. (Below) View from the garden. Construction of steel framework and Thermos slabs, colour washed. Window frames painted grey. A wide folding door leads from the living room to the verandah, and the bedroom opens on to a roomy balcony. Architect, ADOLF RADING, Kronprinzen Ufer, 19/11, Berlin, N.W. 40.

House of Dr. Kriebel, constructed of brick, faced with plaster and coloured grey. (Above) Sleeping balcony, with glazed roof : the supports are placed so as not to interfere with the view. (Below) View from the garden, showing "terraced" construction, arranged in relation to the site.
Architect, ADOLF RADING, Kronprinzenufer, 19/11, Berlin, N.W. 40.

(*Above*) *Row of three houses for single families at Stuttgart-Weissenhof, Germany, seen from the street. Construction of steel framework filled in with slag-stone : walls washed bright blue : steel window frames painted steel blue: doors painted aluminium.* *Architect, MART STAM, Neue Mainzerstr., 18/11, Frankfurt-am-Main.* (*Below*) *Interior of house at Stuttgart* *By means of folding partition doors the rooms can be divided up in various ways. Architect, ADOLF RADING, Berlin.*

*(Above) An interior of one of the houses at Stuttgart   (Below) Another view
of the same houses, seen from the garden.   Architect, MART STAM, Neue Mainzerstrasse, 18/11,
Frankfurt-am-Main, Germany.   (Photos. by courtesy of Akademischer Verlag Dr. Fritz Wedekind
& Co., Stuttgart.)*

Houses at Stuttgart (Above) *View from garden.* (Below) *A living room, with access to kitchen on left, and steps to garden on right. Architect, MART STAM, Neue Mainzerstrasse, 18/11, Frankfurt-am-Main.*

(Above) View of some of the experimental houses at Stuttgart-Weissenhof, Germany, showing block of flats, steel framed, by MIES VAN DER ROHE, Am Karlsbad, 24, Berlin, W. 35.   (Below)   A garden room in one of the dwellings designed by the same architect.

Interior in a house at Stuttgart-Weissenhof, Germany, constructed of poured concrete. Architect, J. J. P. OUD, Avenue Concordia, 28A, Rotterdam. The inexpensive furniture, painted blue, was made by a manufacturer of iron bedsteads : bookshelves painted red.

Block of twenty workmen's flats at The Hook of Holland. (Above) The middle portion of the block, showing gateway leading to small warehouses behind, with shop fronts on either side. (Below) Another view, showing roomy balconies on the first floor, and small gardens in front.
Architect, J. J. P. OUD, Avenue Concordia, 28A, Rotterdam.

*Another view of the workmen's flats   showing corner shop front.   Each block
contains twenty dwellings, with living room, kitchen and one to three bedrooms.   Construction of
reinforced concrete, filled with brick : window frames of steel : walls washed light yellow-grey, doors
and ironwork brilliant blue, library and warehouse doors, bright red.   All shop fronts are under cover
Architect, J. J. P. OUD, Avenue Concordia, 28A, Rotterdam.*

(Above) House at Stuttgart-Weissenhof, Germany, built of hollow bricks, faced with plaster : ceilings of reinforced concrete, and flat roof paved with asphalt. The loggia, opening out of the living room, and the sleeping balcony, are protected by walls in front. (From " Bau und Wohnung," by courtesy of Akademischer Verlag Dr. Fritz Wedekind & Co., Stuttgart.) (Below) House at Falsterbo, Sweden, built of red brick, plastered inside : ceilings of wood : large balconies with iron rails, painted white. On the flat roof is an open fireplace, for use when sitting out on a cold night.
Architect, JOSEF FRANK, Neustiftgasse, 3, Vienna.

(*Above*) *Block of twelve flats at Stuttgart-Weissenhof, Germany, constructed of slabs of pumice concrete.* *The* "*terrace*" *formation provides an open air roof-garden for each flat.* (*Below*) *A living-room in one of the flats, with furniture designed by REINHOLD STOTZ, Barmen.* *Architect, PETER BEHRENS, Genthinerstr., 13 H, Berlin, W.35.*

Interiors in the block of flats at Stuttgart-Weissenhof, Germany, designed by PETER BEHRENS, Berlin. (Above, left) Dressing-cabinet, mirror and seat, designed by Dr. WLACH, Vienna. (Above, right) Dressing-table, mirror and cupboard, designed by WALTER SOBOTKA, Vienna. (Below) Dining-room furniture and fittings in lacquer, designed by PAUL GRIESSER, Bielefeld, Germany.

Block of twelve flats at Stuttgart-Weissenhof, Germany, showing arrangement of roof-terraces.
Architect, PETER BEHRENS, Berlin

A very ingenious device is illustrated in this combined living-room and kitchen. The actual stove and sink can be completely hidden when the sliding frosted glass panels are lowered. Designed by Mies Van der Rohe.

An ingenious method of space-saving is illustrated in this bedroom, designed by Adolf Schneck, for two children. The two beds, and the step leading to the upper bunk, are painted with blue enamel.

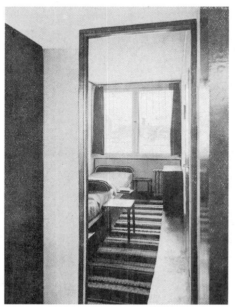

The space in this small sleeping-room is well utilised. The two narrow beds are so placed that the light is behind both sleepers ; the wall is composed of built-in cupboards. Designed by Mies Van der Rohe.

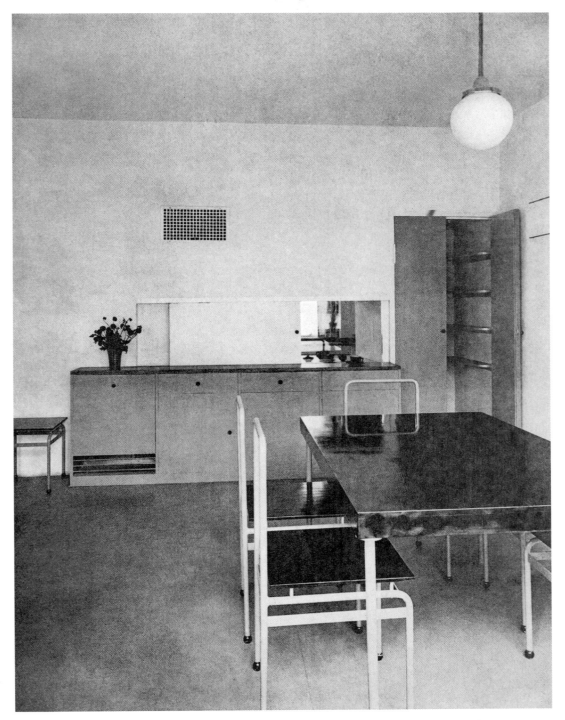

A dining-room designed by J. J. P. Oud shows some very original furniture and simple, but well-proportioned, built-in cupboards.

One wall of this small dining-room is entirely composed of cupboards where all the glass and china can be kept.   A sliding hatch gives access to the kitchen.   Designed by Ludwig Hilberseimer.

This extremely efficient kitchen was designed by Ludwig Hilberseimer. A multitude of cupboards replaces the old-fashioned dresser and chest of drawers.

A kitchen designed by Walter Gropius shows an excellent use of limited space. The drawer knobs are of wood.

A dressing-room of extreme simplicity shows some unusual furniture designed by Lily Reich. The supports of the mirror and the stool in front of it are of bent metal.

Built-in bookshelves and a chair of bent metal are outstanding features of a library designed by Mies Van der Rohe.

Recessed fireplace, illuminated by concealed lighting in the soffit : mantelpiece of Bubinga wood and silver : walls grey and silver. Designed by C. A. RICHTER : made and decorated by THE BATH CABINET MAKERS' CO., LTD., Lower Bristol Road, Bath.

Dining-room for a small flat.   The Coromandel and walnut furniture provides a note of colour which blends with the black and yellow decoration scheme.   The table is in three pieces, of which the central section, when not in use, can be used as a carving table.   Designed for WARING & GILLOW, LTD., Oxford Street, London, W., by S. CHERMAYEFF. The table glass is by R. LALIQUE of Paris

(Above) A rigid economy of detail characterises this bedroom designed by Djo-Bourgeois.   The bed-head is a fixture, and a shelf on the wall replaces the usual bedside table.   Elise Djo-Bourgeois was responsible for the carpet. *(Below)* This very simple but effectual dining-room was designed by Djo-Bourgeois.   In place of a sideboard three shelves are affixed to the wall, the dining-table has a solid base instead of legs and the chairs have solid backs of curved wood.

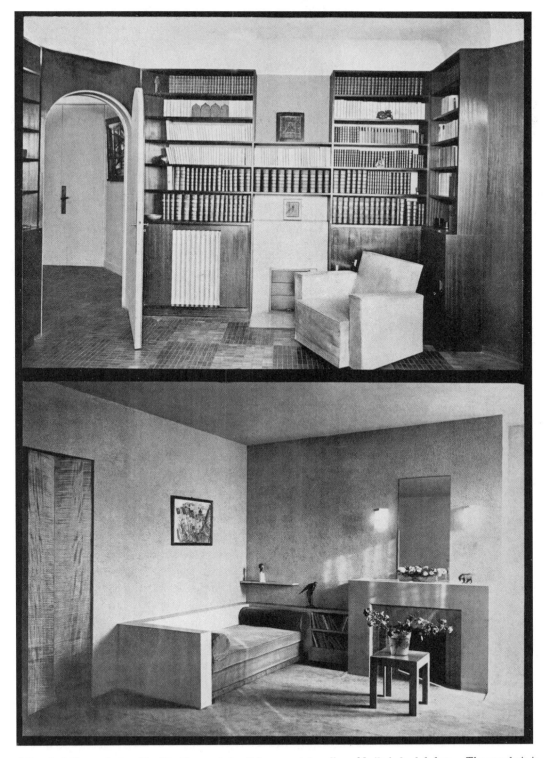

(Above) A library designed by Djo-Bourgeois has light grey-pink walls and built-in bookshelves. The armchair is of natural-coloured leather, and the parquet floor is made of walnut wood. (Below) This charming drawing-room designed by Djo-Bourgeois shows how successful built-in furniture and simple lines can be when the proportions are good.

Bedroom in a flat, with sycamore fittings.   Designed by MICHEL ROUX-SPITZ, Paris.
(Photo Salaün.)

Design for a bedroom by MAURICE DUFRÉNE, Paris. The furniture is in satinwood, the walls distempered ivory colour; an ivory satin counterpane covers the bed, and the carpet is a rich Havana brown.

Boudoir designed by F. & G. SADDIER, Paris : produced by SADDIER & SES FILS. The furniture is executed in undulated sycamore, and the scheme of decoration is carried out in rose colour.

Combined dining-room and living-room designed by F. & G. SADDIER, Paris : executed by SADDIER & SES FILS. The furniture is in walnut wood, and the chair backs are movable, so that they will fit under the table. Sculpture by LAURENT MALCLES

(Above) " *Le Bar sous le Toit* " : *cocktail bar adapted from a mansard room.   Designed by CHARLOTTE PERRIAND, Paris.   (Below) Drawing room suite in sycamore and mahogany, with printed silk curtains. Designed by ERIC BAGGE : produced by PALAIS DE MARBRE (Mercier Frères), Paris.   Silks produced by BOUIX.*

Combined bathroom and dressing room, with fittings of sycamore and Fauquez " Marbrite ":
floor paved with glass paste mosaics.   Designed by MICHEL ROUX-SPITZ, Paris.
(Photo Salaün.)

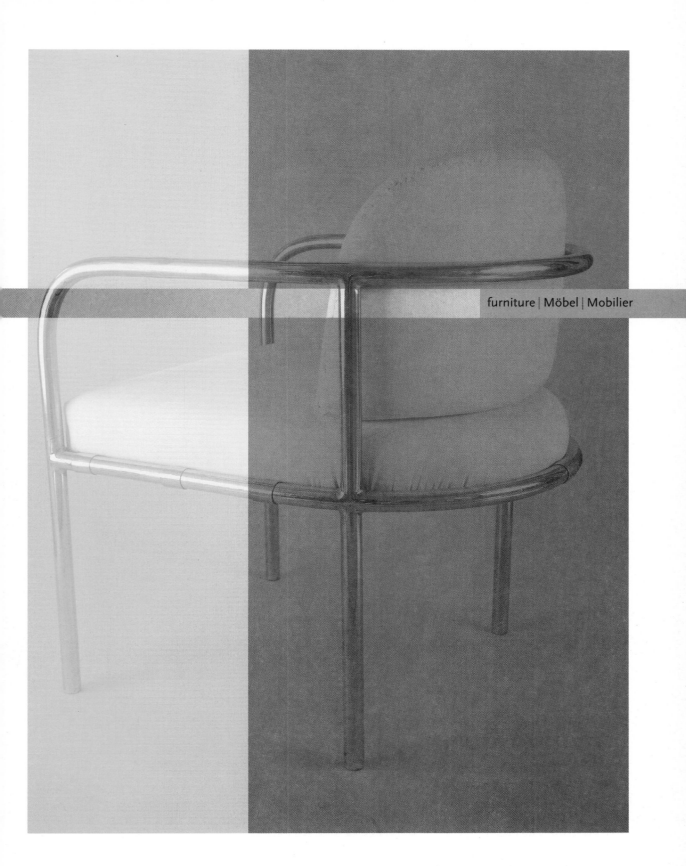

furniture | Möbel | Mobilier

MAHOGANY AND BLACK
SIDEBOARD DESIGNED
BY AMBROSE HEAL,
EXECUTED BY HEAL
AND SON

WALNUT BUREAU DESIGNED BY AMBROSE HEAL
EXECUTED BY HEAL AND SON

COLOUR-COMBED WARDROBE DESIGNED
AND EXECUTED BY HEAL AND SON

WALNUT DINING-ROOM FURNITURE, WITH MOTHER O'PEARL INLAY
DESIGNED BY AMBROSE HEAL, EXECUTED BY HEAL AND SON

OAK FOLDING-TOP DRESSER DESIGNED
BY AMBROSE HEAL, EXECUTED BY HEAL
AND SON

CHESTNUT DRESSER DESIGNED
BY AMBROSE HEAL, EXECUTED
BY HEAL AND SON

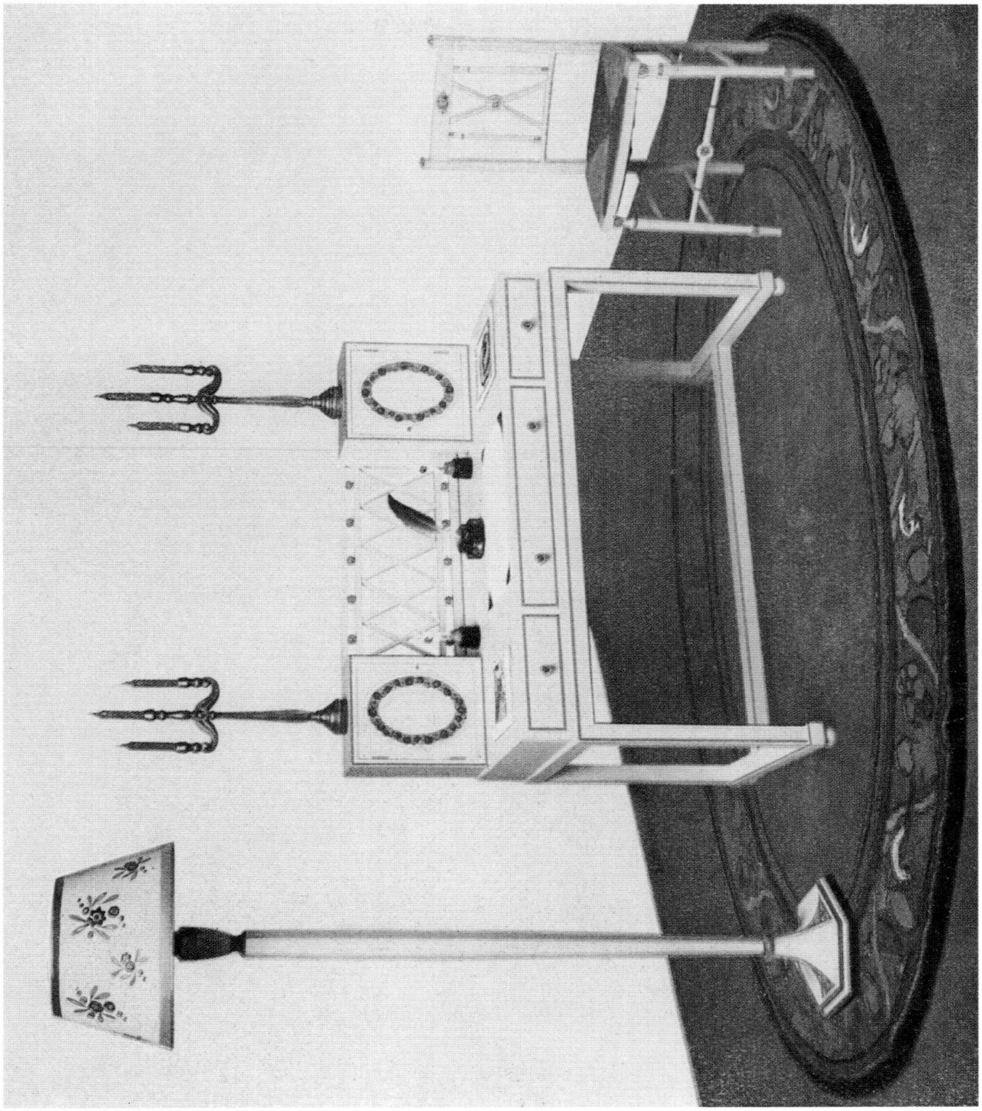

PAINTED FURNITURE DESIGNED BY AMBROSE HEAL, EXECUTED BY HEAL AND

OAK CHEST, WITH CUPBOARD, DESIGNED BY AMBROSE
HEAL, EXECUTED BY HEAL AND SON

SIMPLE WARDROBE BY HEAL AND SON

UNPOLISHED OAK BEDROOM FURNITURE DESIGNED BY AMBROSE HEAL, EXECUTED BY HEAL AND SON

BIRCHWOOD FURNITURE DESIGNED BY HAROLD BERGSTEN

FURNITURE DESIGNED BY KARL NORBERG, EXECUTED BY THE NORDISKA KOMPANIET

BIRCHWOOD CHAIR DESIGNED AND
EXECUTED BY CARL MALMSTEN

BIRCHWOOD CHAIR DESIGNED AND
EXECUTED BY CARL MALMSTEN

BIRCHWOOD CABINET, WITH INLAY, DESIGNED BY CARL
MALMSTEN, EXECUTED BY THE NORDISKA KOMPANIET

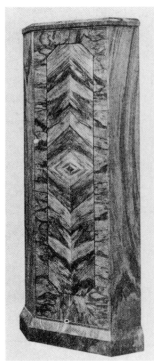

WALNUT FURNITURE, WITH EBONY INLAY, BY LIBERTY AND COMPANY

WALNUT DINING-TABLE, WITH EBONY INLAY, BY LIBERTY AND COMPANY

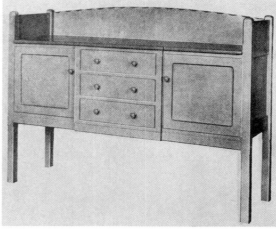

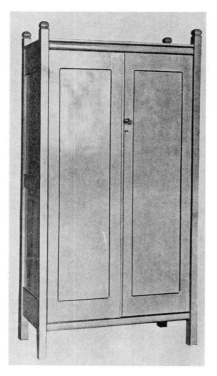

PAINTED FURNITURE DESIGNED BY PERCY A. WELLS, EXECUTED BY OETZMANN AND COMPANY

FURNITURE IN ENGLISH OAK DESIGNED AND EXECUTED BY P. WAALS

TEAK SIDEBOARD DE-
SIGNED AND EXE-
CUTED BY JOSCELYNE'S
OF JOHANNESBURG.

TEAK DRESSING-TABLE
AND SEAT DESIGNED
AND EXECUTED BY
JOSCELYNE'S, OF JO-
HANNESBURG

TEAK SIDEBOARD DESIGNED
AND EXECUTED BY JOSCELYNE'S
OF JOHANNESBURG.

TEAK DRESSING-TABLE DESIGNED
AND EXECUTED BY JOSCELYNE'S
CF JOHANNESBURG.

OAK BOOKCASE
DESIGNED BY
PROFESSOR OTTO
PRUTSCHER, EXE-
CUTED BY J. W.
MÜLLER

OAK CABINET DESIGNED BY PROF. OTTO
PRUTSCHER. EXECUTED BY J. W. MÜLLER

CABINET DESIGNED BY PROF. OTTO PRUTSCHER, EXECUTED
BY J. KARASEK

FURNITURE DESIGNED AND EXECUTED BY JACQUES RUHLMANN

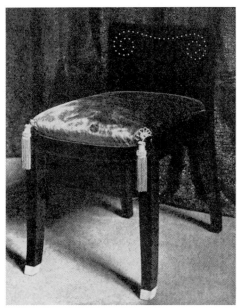

FURNITURE DESIGNED AND EXECUTED BY JACQUES RUHLMANN

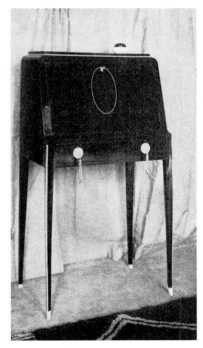

FURNITURE DESIGNED AND EXECUTED BY JACQUES RUHLMANN

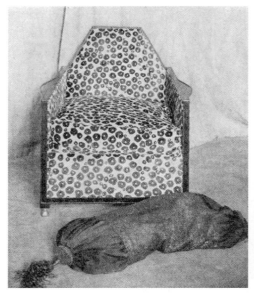

FURNITURE DESIGNED AND EXE-
CUTED BY JACQUES RUHLMANN

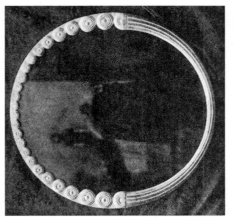

MIRROR WITH CARVED WOOD FRAME, GILDED

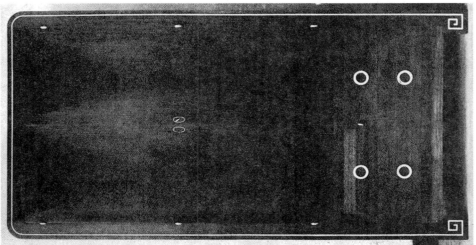

CUPBOARD IN AMARANTH AND IVORY

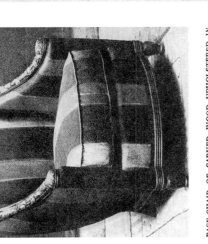

EASY-CHAIR OF CARVED WOOD UPHOLSTERED IN
BLACK AND GOLD

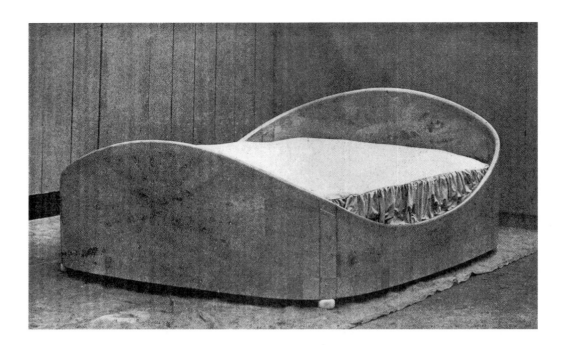

BEDSTEAD AND CONVERTIBLE EASY-CHAIRS DESIGNED AND EXECUTED BY ANDRÉ GROULT

SMALL SIDEBOARD WITH DRAWERS, IN SYCAMORE AND AMARANTH, DESIGNED AND
EXECUTED BY FERNAND NATHAN

CHAIRS DESIGNED AND EXECUTED BY FERNAND NATHAN

BOUDOIR DESIGNED AND EXECUTED BY ERIC **BAGGE** AND BERNARD HUGUET

INTERIOR DESIGNED AND EXECUTED BY M. GALLEREY

SETTEE DESIGNED BY MAURICE DUFRÈNE

FURNITURE, LAMP, HANGING AND RUG BY HEAL AND SON ; MIRROR AND BOX DESIGNED BY J. BORIE, EXECUTED BY
THE CANAL WORKSHOP ; WINDOW CASEMENT BY WAINWRIGHT AND WARING

PAINTED FURNITURE DESIGNED BY J. BORIE, EXECUTED BY THE CANAL WORKSHOP; LAMP, RUG AND TEA SET BY HEAL AND SON; PLAQUE BY CARTER, STABLER AND ADAMS; CRETONNE DESIGNED BY MINNIE MᶜLEISH FOR W. FOXTON

ENTOMOLOGICAL CABINET IN ITALIAN WALNUT, DESIGNED BY CHARLES SPOONER, EXECUTED BY G. T. BATTEN
(L.C.C CENTRAL SCHOOL OF ARTS AND CRAFTS)

INTERIORS DESIGNED BY SHIRLEY B. WAINWRIGHT

GARDEN SEAT IN TERRA-COTTA DESIGNED AND EXECUTED BY WILLEM C. BROUWER, LEIDERDORP

GARDEN FURNITURE IN STONE AND TERRA-COTTA DESIGNED
AND EXECUTED BY WILLEM C. BROUWER, LEIDERDORP

MAHOGANY BEDROOM SUITE TREATED WITH PIGMENTS
OF TWO TONES OF BLUE. DESIGNED AND EXECUTED
BY LIBERTY AND CO., LTD., REGENT STREET. LONDON

CHAIR DESIGNED BY FERNAND PETIT, TABLE BY LOUIS GOVAERTS. EXECUTED BY VANDERBORGHT FRÈRES, BRUSSELS

SILVER CABINET IN ITALIAN WALNUT. DESIGNED BY SUTRO MERTRIEDERAND, EXECUTED BY A. POSSENBACHER, MUNICH

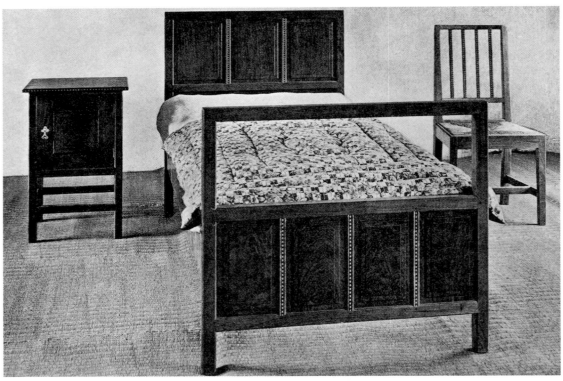

BEDROOM FURNITURE IN ENGLISH WALNUT. DESIGNED AND EXECUTED BY PETER WAALS, CHALFORD, GLOUCESTERSHIRE (SUCCESSOR TO THE LATE E. W. GIMSON)

WARDROBE IN ENGLISH WALNUT, CHAIRS AND WRITING CABINET IN
ENGLISH OAK. DESIGNED AND EXECUTED BY PETER WAALS, CHAL-
FORD, GLOUCESTERSHIRE (SUCCESSOR TO THE LATE E. W. GIMSON)

SILVER CUPBOARD ON STAND AND WASHSTAND IN ENGLISH
WALNUT. DESIGNED AND EXECUTED BY PETER WAALS, CHALFORD
GLOUCESTERSHIRE (SUCCESSOR TO THE LATE E. W. GIMSON)

WRITING TABLE AND CHAIR IN WALNUT, CHESTS
IN BROWN OAK. DESIGNED AND EXECUTED
BY A ROMNEY GREEN, CHRISTCHURCH, HANTS.

OVAL SPRING-LID BOX, TWO CARVED AND PAINTED
FRAMES AND BEDSTEAD IN ENGLISH OAK. DESIGNED
AND EXECUTED BY STANLEY PARKER, LETCHWORTH

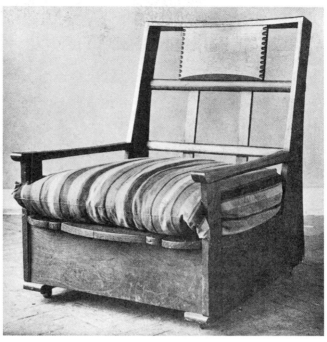

MUSIC-STAND, TABLE AND CARVED CHEST IN ENGLISH
OAK, ARM-CHAIR IN ENGLISH ELM. DESIGNED AND
EXECUTED BY STANLEY PARKER, LETCHWORTH

BEDROOM FURNITURE DESIGNED AND EXECUTED BY
HEAL & SON, LTD., TOTTENHAM COURT ROAD, LONDON

"WEATHERED OAK" SECTIONAL SECRETARY BOOKCASE
BY GUNN AND COMPANY

"WEATHERED OAK" SIDEBOARD WITH MAHOGANY MOULDINGS. DESIGNED
AND EXECUTED BY HEAL AND SON, LTD., TOTTENHAM COURT ROAD, LONDON

"WEATHERED OAK" SIDEBOARD AND FIGURED MAHOGANY DRESSING - CHEST AND WASHSTAND
DESIGNED AND EXECUTED BY HEAL AND SON, LTD., TOTTENHAM COURT ROAD, LONDON

WRITING-DESK IN WALNUT ON EBONISED STAND WITH ROWLEY PANEL ON FRONT; RED LACQUER AND GILT
DRESSING-TABLE; BOOKCASE IN WALNUT, EBONY AND GILT. DESIGNED BY W. J. PALMER-JONES, 11, BUCK-
INGHAM STREET, LONDON. THE WRITING-DESK WAS DESIGNED FOR JERNINGHAMS, LTD.

DRESSING-TABLE IN AMARANTH WITH SILVER
FILLETS. DESIGNED AND EXECUTED BY "MAM"
(MICHEL DUFET AND LOUIS BUREAU), PARIS

DRAWING-ROOM FURNITURE   DESIGNED AND EXECUTED BY FRANCIS JOURDAIN, PARIS

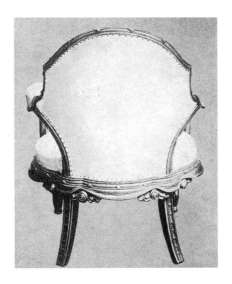

CARVED AND GILDED ARM-CHAIR, UPHOLSTERED IN BEAUVAIS TAPESTRY. DESIGNED AND EXECUTED BY PAUL FOLLOT, PARIS, FOR THE STATE

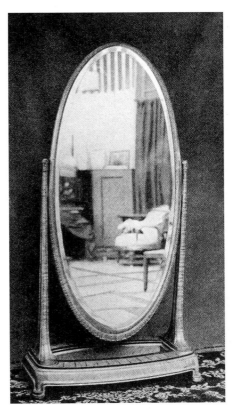

CHEVAL-GLASS INLAID WITH AMARANTH, EBONY AND HOLLY. DESIGNED AND EXECUTED BY PAUL FOLLOT, PARIS

CARVED AND LACQUERED DRESSING-TABLE WITH TWO DRAWERS OPENING AT SIDES. DESIGNED AND EXECUTED BY PAUL FOLLOT PARIS

SIDEBOARD INLAID WITH IVORY AND PEWTER.
DESIGNED AND EXECUTED BY " MAM " (MICHEL DUFET AND LOUIS BUREAU), PARIS

EBONY DRESSING-TABLE DESIGNED AND EXECUTED BY LOUIS SUE ET
MARE, COMPAGNIE DES ARTS FRANÇAIS, PARIS

CARVED AND GILDED MAPLEWOOD CABINET
DESIGNED AND EXECUTED BY " MAM " (MICHEL
DUFET AND LOUIS BUREAU), PARIS

FURNITURE DESIGNED AND
EXECUTED BY A. FABRE, PARIS

CREAM-COLOURED DRESSING-TABLE DE-
SIGNED BY PROF. OSKAR KAUFMANN, BERLIN

DRESSING-TABLE IN GREY LIME-WOOD. DESIGNED AND EXECUTED
BY " MAM " (MICHEL DUFET AND LOUIS BUREAU), PARIS

ENAMELLED PINEWOOD KITCHEN FURNITURE DESIGNED BY FR. KADACH, FOR " HAUSRAT," BERLIN

IVORY PAINTED BEDROOM FURNITURE DESIGNED AND EXECUTED BY PROF. FRITZ SPANNAGEL
KARLSRUHE. PAINTED ORNAMENTATION BY HERTA VON GUMPPENBERG

IVORY PAINTED BEDROOM FURNITURE DESIGNED AND EXECUTED BY PROF. FRITZ SPANNAGEL, KARLSRUHE

SIDEBOARD DESIGNED BY RUDOLF BRÜNING, DÜSSELDORF

BEDROOM FURNITURE DESIGNED BY RUDOLF BRÜNING, DÜSSELDORF

COUCH UPHOLSTERED IN GREY. DESIGNED BY PROF. FRITZ SPANNAGEL, KARLSRUHE
EXECUTED BY THE DEUTSCHE WERKSTÄTTEN, MUNICH

SIDEBOARD OF CAUCASIAN WALNUT. DESIGNED BY PROF. FRITZ SPANNAGEL, KARLSRUHE, EXECUTED BY GROSSBERGER
AND ZAPPOLD, NUREMBERG. INLAY DESIGNED BY PROF. ALBERT HAUEISEN, KARLSRUHE, EXECUTED BY HEINRICH
MAYBACH, KARLSRUHE

CHAIR AND WRITING TABLE DESIGNED AND EXECUTED BY C. MALMSTEN, STOCKHOLM

OAK CUPBOARD WITH DRAWERS, DESIGNED BY PETER
WAALS, CHESTNUT HOUSE, CHALFORD, GLOUCESTERSHIRE

OFFICE CHAIR IN WALNUT

WALNUT CHAIR

HALL CHAIR IN OAK

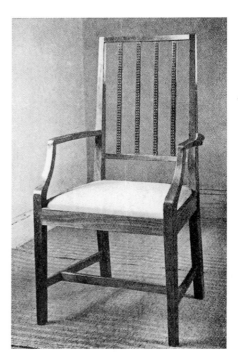

ARMCHAIR IN WALNUT

FOUR CHAIRS DESIGNED AND EXECUTED BY PETER WAALS, CHESTNUT HOUSE, CHALFORD, GLOUCESTERSHIRE

CHAIR, LOW STOOL AND EXTENDING TABLE IN ENGLISH OAK, DESIGNED AND EXECUTED BY A. ROMNEY GREEN, CHRISTCHURCH, HANTS.

"TOKEN" COTTAGE BEDSTEAD, STOOL AND DOWRY CHEST IN DARK TEAK AND FLOWERED OAK.
DESIGNED AND EXECUTED BY BETTY JOEL, HAYLING ISLAND, HANTS. MIRRORS BY A. J. ROWLEY,
CHURCH STREET, KENSINGTON

TABLE AND CHAIR OF UNPOLISHED ENGLISH WALNUT DESIGNED BY CHAS. HOLDEN, OF ADAMS, HOLDEN AND
PEARSON, AND EXECUTED BY WARING AND GILLOW, LTD., OXFORD STREET, LONDON

CLOCK OF QUARTERED ENGLISH OAK WITH DULL SILVERED DIAL, SIMPLE DRESSER AND SHELVES IN ENGLISH OAK AND THREE STOOLS IN ENGLISH OAK WITH TOPS OF HIDE. DESIGNED BY GORDON RUSSELL AND EXECUTED BY RUSSELL AND SONS, BROADWAY, WORCESTERSHIRE

A SIMPLE OAK DRESSER, WITH WROT IRON DROP HANDLES, AND A DINING-TABLE IN ENGLISH OAK. DESIGNED BY GORDON RUSSELL AND MADE BY RUSSELL AND SONS, BROADWAY, WORCESTERSHIRE

DRESSING TABLE, STOOL, MIRROR AND CANDLESTICKS
IN FINELY FIGURED ENGLISH WALNUT, LINED WITH
CEDAR, DESIGNED BY GORDON RUSSELL AND MADE
BY RUSSELL & SONS, BROADWAY, WORCESTERSHIRE

GATE-LEG TABLE IN ENGLISH BROWN OAK, WITH OCTAGONAL TOP AND TWO CUPBOARDS, AND A BENCH OF ENGLISH OAK WITH SEAT OF INTERLACED HIDE. DESIGNED BY GORDON RUSSELL AND EXECUTED BY RUSSELL AND SONS, BROADWAY, WORCESTERSHIRE

CHEST-ON-STAND IN ENGLISH OAK, LINED WITH CEDAR, HANDLES OF FORGED BRASS, ENGLISH OAK STOOL WITH TOP OF INTERLACED RUBBER AND LEATHER AND AN ENGLISH OAK STOOL, WITH WAGON CHAMFERING, DESIGNED BY GORDON RUSSELL AND EXECUTED BY RUSSELL AND SONS, BROADWAY, WORCESTERSHIRE

CHEST OF DRAWERS IN CHERRY WOOD DESIGNED BY KARL HOFMANN AND FELIX AUGENFELD, VIENNA, AND EXECUTED BY KARL SCHREITL

SIDEBOARD DESIGNED BY DR. JOSEF FRANK

CABINET DESIGNED BY DR. OSKAR WLACH,
ARCHITECT, BERLIN. DECORATION BY FRAU
ANNY SCHROEDER EHRENFEST, VIENNA

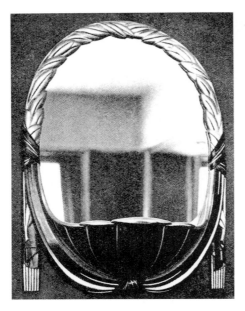

MIRROR FRAME IN BLACK AND GOLD DESIGNED AND
EXECUTED BY LOUIS SÜE ET MARE, PARIS

BABY'S PERAMBULATOR, ROYAL BLUE LACQUER AND PRINTED
MUSLIN DESIGNED BY " MARTINE " (PAUL POIRET) PARIS

WIRELESS INSTALLATION FOR DRAWING-ROOM DESIGNED BY PHILIPPE PETIT AND REVÉ JOUBERT, 19 RUE DE LA
MADELEINE, PARIS

TOILET TABLE OF POLISHED ASH AND SYCAMORE, INLAID IVORY AND EBONY, BY MARCEL CHARPENTIER, PARIS

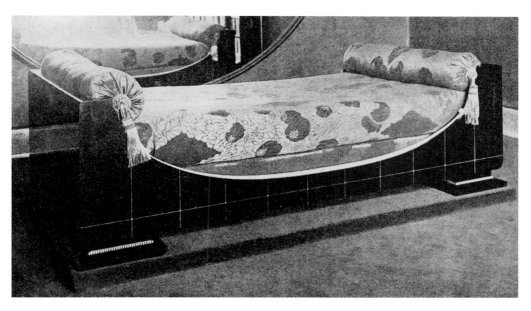

COUCH OF MACASSAR EBONY, INLAID WITH IVORY AND UPHOLSTERED IN SILK DAMASK DESIGNED BY J. KUHLMANN, PARIS

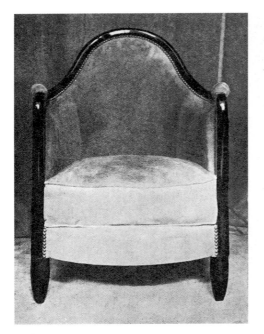

ARMCHAIRS UPHOLSTERED IN GREY LEATHER AND IN PRINTED LINEN " FABRIC MARTINE " DESIGNED AND EXECUTED BY " MARTINE " (PAUL POIRET), PARIS

GILT ARMCHAIR DESIGNED AND EXECUTED BY LOUIS SÜE ET MARE, PARIS. UPHOLSTERED IN BEAUVAIS TAPESTRY DESIGNED BY M. TAQUOY, PARIS

SMOKE-ROOM CHAIR, DESIGNED AND EXECUTED BY DOMINIQUE, PARIS
Upholstery: Orange silk inside, black silk outside; pedestal and feet of ebony with pewter decoration

BOOKCASE AND TABLE IN POLISHED ASH. DESIGNED
AND EXECUTED BY MARCEL CHARPENTIER, PARIS

BOOKCASE OF EBONY INLAID WITH IVORY, CABINET OF "LOUPE D'AMBOIRE" INLAID WITH IVORY AND DINING-TABLE OF POLISHED OAK DESIGNED AND EXECUTED BY J. RUHLMANN, PARIS

CHEST IN OAK DESIGNED BY A. J. KROPHOLLER, B.N.A., WASSENAAR, HOLLAND
(*Plaques by Mendes da Costa, " Adam and Eve before and after the Fall." Corner ornaments—owls*)

OCCASIONAL CHAIR AND TEA WAGON WITH REMOVABLE TRAY DESIGNED BY H. S. TOMPKINS FOR JOSCELYNES LTD.,
JOHANNESBURG

DRESSING TABLE AND MIRROR OF ENGLISH WALNUT. DESIGNED BY
S. GORDON RUSSELL, AND EXECUTED BY RUSSELL AND SONS, BROADWAY,
WORCESTERSHIRE

CHEST OF DRAWERS IN ENGLISH OAK. DESIGNED BY
S. GORDON RUSSELL, AND EXECUTED BY RUSSELL AND
SONS, BROADWAY, WORCESTERSHIRE

DRESSING TABLE AND LOOKING GLASS OF
MAHOGANY. DESIGNED BY C. SPOONER, EYOT
COTTAGE, CHISWICK MALL, LONDON

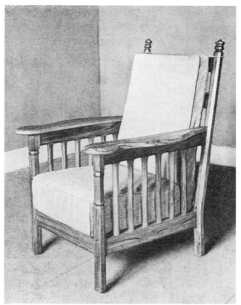

CHEST ON STAND IN WALNUT ; CHAIR IN ENGLISH WALNUT ; DRESSING TABLE AND STANDING MIRROR IN ENGLISH OAK ; PEDESTAL CUPBOARD, WITH BOOKSHELVES OVER, IN ENGLISH WALNUT. DESIGNED BY S. GORDON RUSSELL, AND EXECUTED BY RUSSELL AND SONS, BROADWAY, WORCESTERSHIRE

BEDSTEAD AND DRESSER IN WALNUT. DESIGNED AND EXECUTED BY A. ROMNEY GREEN, CHRISTCHURCH, HANTS.

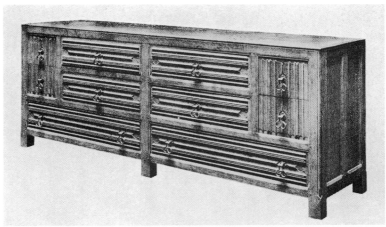

TWO CHESTS IN ENGLISH OAK.   DESIGNED AND EXECUTED BY LIBERTY AND CO. LTD.,
REGENT STREET, LONDON

DRESSER IN ENGLISH OAK. DESIGNED BY E. ARTHUR
BROWN, OF CROSSLEY AND BROWN, GOLDERS GREEN

ARM CHAIR IN ENGLISH OAK. DESIGNED,
EXECUTED AND CARVED BY DOUGLAS CROSSLEY,
OF CROSSLEY AND BROWN, GOLDERS GREEN

SIDEBOARD IN MAHOGANY. DESIGNED BY E. ARTHUR BROWN, OF CROSSLEY
AND BROWN, 11, TEMPLARS PARADE, GOLDERS GREEN, LONDON

TABLE IN ENGLISH OAK.   DESIGNED AND EXECUTED BY DOUGLAS CROSSLEY, OF
CROSSLEY AND BROWN, GOLDERS GREEN

CABINET SIDEBOARD IN ENGLISH OAK, WITH FITTINGS OF WROUGHT IRON.   DESIGNED
BY E. ARTHUR BROWN, OF CROSSLEY AND BROWN, 11, TEMPLARS PARADE, GOLDERS
GREEN, LONDON

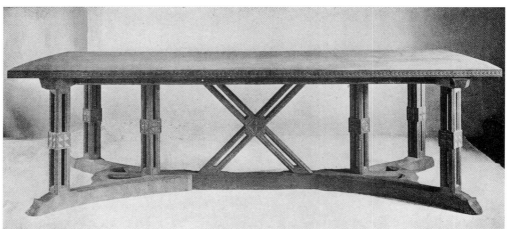

BUREAU OF ENGLISH WALNUT AND CEREMONIAL TABLE OF OAK. DESIGNED AND EXECUTED BY PETER WAALS, CHALFORD, GLOS.

WRITING CABINET OF ENGLISH WALNUT. DESIGNED
AND EXECUTED BY PETER WAALS, CHALFORD, GLOS.

DRESSING TABLE OF "AMBOINE" AND EBONY.
DESIGNED BY PIERRE CHAREAU, PARIS

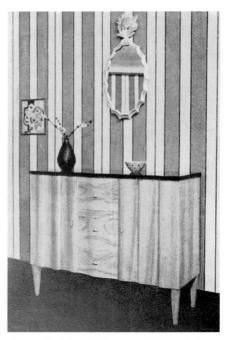

CHEST OF DRAWERS. DESIGNED BY MME.
CHAUCHET-GUILLERÉ, OF THE ATELIER,
PRIMAVERA, PARIS

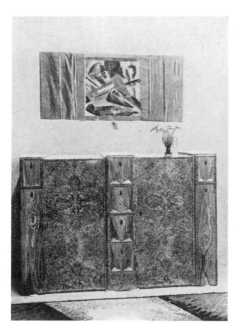

CHEST OF DRAWERS IN THUJA AND VIOLET
EBONY. DESIGNED BY PIERRE CHAREAU, PARIS

CHEST INLAID WITH EBONY. DESIGNED BY
POUSSET, OF THE "ATELIER DE LA MAÎTRISE,"
PARIS

DECORATED CHEST IN COROMANDEL.
DESIGNED BY MME. CLAUDE-LÉVY, OF
THE " ATELIER PRIMAVERA," PARIS

SIDEBOARD WITH MOTIF IN CARVED MAHOGANY. DESIGNED AND EXECUTED BY
EMILE BERNAUX, PARIS

DINING ROOM SUITE IN OAK. DESIGNED BY ANDRADA, OF THE "ATELIER DE LA MAÎTRISE," PARIS

INLAID WALNUT CABINET. DESIGNED BY MARCEL BOVIS, FOR THE POMONE BON MARCHÉ, PARIS

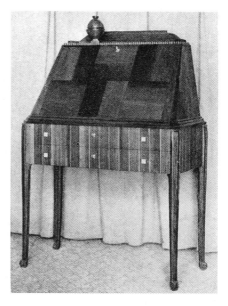

WRITING BUREAU IN ROSEWOOD. DESIGNED AND EXECUTED BY " DIM," PARIS

OAK JEWEL CABINET WITH IVORY HANDLES. DESIGNED AND EXECUTED BY JACQUES RUHLMANN, PARIS

CHEST OF AMBOYNA WITH IVORY ORNAMENTATION. DESIGNED AND EXECUTED BY JACQUES RUHLMANN, PARIS

UPHOLSTERED CHAIR DESIGNED AND EXECUTED BY
J. AND M. LELEU, BOULOGNE-SUR-MER, FRANCE

ARMCHAIR IN SATIN. DESIGNED AND EXECUTED BY
FRANCIS JOURDAIN, PARIS

UPHOLSTERED ARMCHAIR. DESIGNED AND EXECUTED
BY PIERRE CHAREAU, PARIS

ARMCHAIR WITH SLOPING BACK. DESIGNED AND
EXECUTED BY PIERRE CHAREAU, PARIS

CHEST IN VIOLET EBONY AND GILDED
MIRROR. DESIGNED AND EXECUTED BY
MONTAGNAC, PARIS

SIMPLE WRITING TABLE AND SMALL MIRROR IN OAK STAINED BROWN AND BLACK; AND SIMPLE NURSERY FURNITURE IN STAINED OAK. DESIGNED BY WILLEM PENAAT, AMSTERDAM, AND EXECUTED BY METZ AND CO., AMSTERDAM, HOLLAND

WARDROBE, BOOKCASE, MIRROR, TABLE AND ARMCHAIR IN OAK, STAINED BROWN AND BLACK.   SIMPLE
FURNITURE DESIGNED BY WILLEM PENAAT, AMSTERDAM, AND EXECUTED BY METZ AND CO., AMSTERDAM,
HOLLAND

FURNITURE DESIGNED BY JENS MOELLER JENSEN,
AND EXECUTED BY " MODEL-BOHAVE," COPENHAGEN,
DENMARK

GIRL'S STUDY IN RED AKUMÉ. DESIGNED BY JAC. VAN DEN BOSCH, AND EXECUTED BY
'T BINNENHUIS, AMSTERDAM, HOLLAND

WALNUT SIDEBOARD. DESIGNED BY KARL HOFMANN AND FELIX AUGENFELD, ARCHITECTS, AND EXECUTED BY KARL SCHREITL, VIENNA, AUSTRIA

CHEST IN CHERRY AND PEARWOOD. DESIGNED AND EXECUTED BY KARL SCHREITL AND HANS PETER, VIENNA, AUSTRIA

WALNUT WARDROBE. DESIGNED BY HUGO GORGE, AND EXECUTED BY R. LORENZ, VIENNA, AUSTRIA

WRITING DESK IN CHERRY WOOD. DESIGNED BY
HUGO GORGE, AND EXECUTED BY R. LORENZ,
VIENNA, AUSTRIA

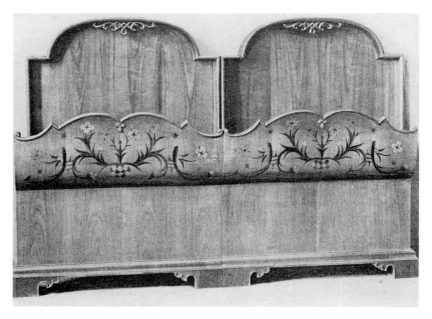

BEDSTEAD IN CHERRY WOOD. DESIGNED BY JOSEF GRAF, BUDAPEST, HUNGARY

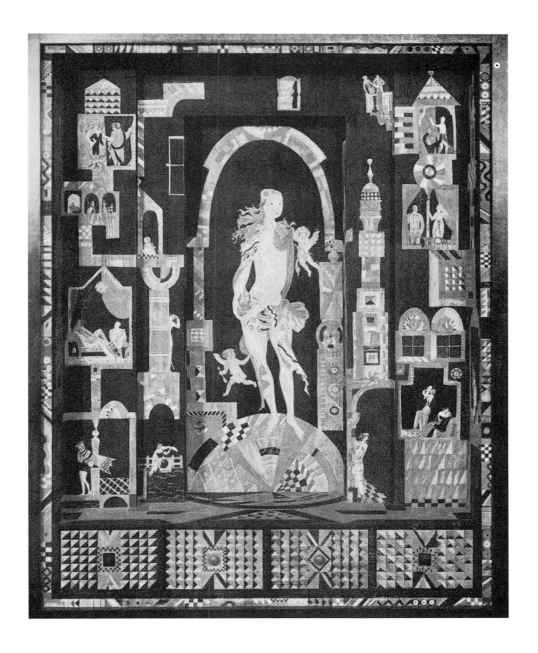

MARQUETRY PANEL IN VARIOUS BROWN
WOODS FOR CUPBOARD DOOR. DESIGNED
AND EXECUTED BY MARIA STRAUSS-LIKARZ,
VIENNA, AUSTRIA

DRESSING TABLE AND MIRROR, CHEST OF DRAWERS, AND BEDSIDE TABLE IN
CHERRYWOOD, INLAID WITH WALNUT AND BOXWOOD. DESIGNED BY S. GORDON
RUSSELL, AND EXECUTED BY RUSSELL AND SONS, BROADWAY, WORCESTERSHIRE

WRITING CABINET IN CHERRYWOOD,
WITH HANDLES OF EBONY AND LABUR-
NUM. DESIGNED BY S. GORDON RUSSELL,
AND EXECUTED BY RUSSELL AND SONS,
BROADWAY, WORCESTERSHIRE. (*Lowest
drawer extended with front let down forms desk*)

OAK FALL FRONT WRITING CABINET.   DESIGNED BY S. GORDON
RUSSELL, AND EXECUTED BY RUSSELL AND SONS, BROADWAY,
WORCESTERSHIRE
(Inlaid ebony and yew, with veneered
interior and brass fittings)

OAK TABLE.   DESIGNED BY SHIRLEY B. WAINWRIGHT, FINCHLEY, LONDON

BEDROOM FURNITURE IN WEATHERED OAK WITH LIGHTLY CARVED EBONISED MOULDING. DESIGNED
AND EXECUTED BY HEAL AND SON, LTD., 195 TO 198, TOTTENHAM COURT ROAD, LONDON

PIANOFORTE BY GABRIEL GAVEAU.   EXECUTED BY "DOMINIQUE," PARIS

WARDROBE IN MACASSAR EBONY AND ARMCHAIR UPHOLSTERED IN LEATHER.   DESIGNED BY
LOUIS SOGNOT AND EXECUTED BY THE ATELIER PRIMAVERA, PARIS

CABINET IN THUJA WOOD WITH MARQUETRY DECORATION.
DESIGNED BY MAURICE DUFRÈNE, AND EXECUTED BY THE
ATELIER DE LA MAÎTRISE, PARIS

COUCH IN ROSEWOOD, UPHOLSTERED IN DAMASK. DESIGNED AND EXECUTED BY
JACQUES RUHLMANN, PARIS

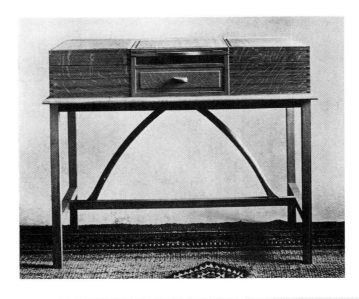

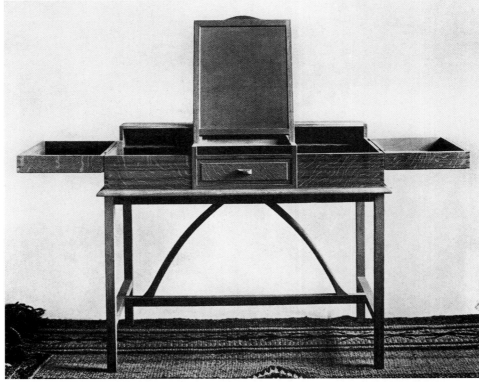

FOLDING DRESSING TABLE, CLOSED AND OPEN. DESIGNED AND EXECUTED BY PETER WAALS, CHALFORD, GLOUCESTERSHIRE

GROUP OF FURNITURE IN "DRY-
TONED," BRITISH COLUMBIA HEM-
LOCK AND SEQUOIA. FROM A PEN
DRAWING BY W. J. PALMER JONES,
11, BUCKINGHAM STREET, LONDON

SIMPLE FURNITURE IN OAK, STAINED BROWN AND BLACK. DESIGNED BY WILLEM PENAAT,
AMSTERDAM, AND EXECUTED BY METZ AND COMPANY, AMSTERDAM, HOLLAND
(*top of chest—lower plate—in rosewood*)

CABINET WITH MARQUETRY PANELS.
DESIGNED BY V. SURJÉ, AND EXECUTED
BY THE DEUTSCHE WERKSTÄTTEN, A.G.,
MUNICH, GERMANY

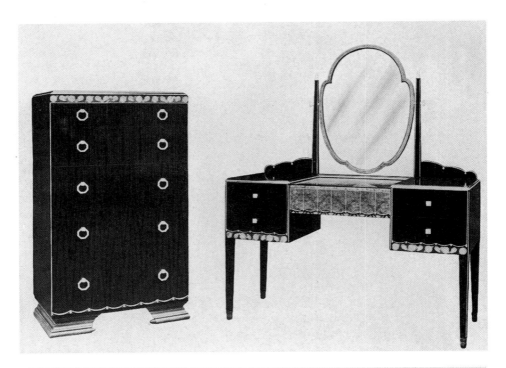

FURNITURE DESIGNED AND EXECUTED BY B. COHEN AND SONS, LTD., 1-19, CURTAIN
ROAD, LONDON

*(Above) Chest and dressing-table in Macassar ebony and amboyna, with fine
coloured marquetry bandings. (Below) Chest and dressing-table in figured
walnut and amboyna with marquetry motifs*

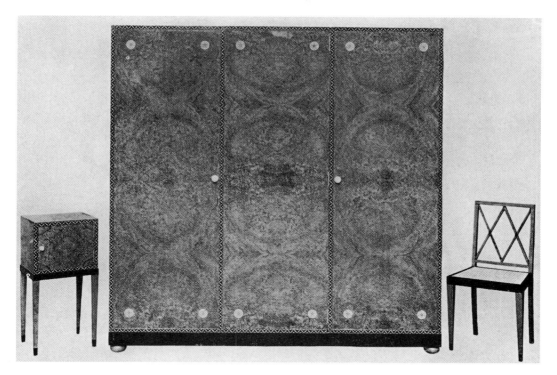

FURNITURE DESIGNED BY C. A. RICHTER, EXECUTED BY BATH ARTCRAFT, LIMITED, BATH
Bedroom suite in amboyna walnut, mogador and mother-of-pearl inlay

"TOKEN" FURNITURE — CEDAR-LINED
WARDROBE AND OVAL MIRROR
DRESSING-TABLE IN BLACK WAL-
NUT. DESIGNED AND MADE BY BETTY
JOEL, 177, SLOANE STREET, LONDON

WASH-HAND STAND AT STRAFFORD LODGE,
WEYBRIDGE. DESIGNED BY JOSEPH
EMBERTON, A.R.I.B.A., 150, REGENT STREET,
LONDON   *Sycamore inlaid*
walnut with glass back and top.   Toilet ware of
green opaque glass

SMALL CABINET IN WALNUT DESIGNED AND EXECUTED
BY PETER WAALS, CHALFONT, GLOUCESTERSHIRE

TWO ARMCHAIRS IN WALNUT DESIGNED AND EXECUTED BY PETER WAALS, CHALFONT,
GLOUCESTERSHIRE

PLATE CUPBOARD IN WALNUT. DE-
SIGNED AND EXECUTED BY PETER
WAALS, CHALFONT, GLOUCESTER

WEATHERED OAK CIRCULAR TOP TABLE (3 FT. 9 IN. DIAMETER) ON CENTRE LEG.
DESIGNED BY AMBROSE HEAL, MADE BY HEAL AND SON, LTD., TOTTENHAM COURT
ROAD, LONDON

MAHOGANY SIDEBOARD DESIGNED BY S. GORDON RUSSELL; EXECUTED BY RUSSELL AND SONS,
BROADWAY, WORCESTERSHIRE

WALNUT EASY CHAIR, WITH LOOSE SEAT AND BACK COVERED IN HIDE ; AND SIMPLE OAK BUREAU, DESIGNED BY S. GORDON RUSSELL, EXECUTED BY RUSSELL AND SONS, BROADWAY, WORCESTERSHIRE

LARGE OAK DOUBLE GATE-LEG TABLE, DESIGNED BY S. GORDON RUSSELL AND EXECUTED BY RUSSELL AND SONS, BROADWAY, WORCESTERSHIRE

WARDROBE, DRESSING-TABLE AND CHEST
OF DRAWERS (LINED CEDAR) IN ENGLISH
OAK WITH HANDLES OF BOG OAK, DE-
SIGNED BY S. GORDON RUSSELL AND
EXECUTED BY RUSSELL & SONS, BROAD-
WAY, WORCESTERSHIRE

WARDROBE IN ENGLISH OAK
DESIGNED AND MADE BY
ERIC SHARPE, CHRISTCHURCH,
HAMPSHIRE

SIDEBOARD DESIGNED AND EXECUTED BY H. S. TOMPKINS, JOHANNESBURG, SOUTH AFRICA

HALL TABLE DESIGNED BY CHARLES STRYJENSKI, EXECUTED BY MARTENS ET DAAB, WARSAW

DINING-ROOM CHAIR IN BURMAN TEAK (OILED) DESIGNED AND EXECUTED BY H. S. TOMPKINS, JOHANNESBURG, SOUTH AFRICA

CHEST OF DRAWERS IN ROSEWOOD, DESIGNED AND EXECUTED BY "DIM," PARIS

BEDSTEAD IN ROSEWOOD DESIGNED BY PIERRE CHAREAU, PARIS. MOVEABLE BED-TABLE

GILDED COUCH UPHOLSTERED IN "CAMBO" FABRIC, DESIGNED AND EXECUTED BY "DOMINIQUE," PARIS

UPHOLSTERED CHAIRS, DESIGNED AND EXECUTED BY J. AND M. LELEU, BOULOGNE-SUR-MER

COUCH DESIGNED BY RENÉ HERBST, 4, CHATEAUBRIAND, PARIS
Framework in cherrywood

CHAIR DESIGNED BY BUKHALTER AND
EXECUTED BY PIERRE CHAREAU, PARIS

SIDEBOARD IN ROSEWOOD, DESIGNED AND EXECUTED BY P. P. MONTAGNAC, PARIS

COUCH IN WALNUT UPHOLSTERED IN YELLOW VELVET, CURTAIN IN GREY AND GREEN; DESIGNED AND
EXECUTED BY PIERRE CHAREAU, PARIS

SIDEBOARD IN ROSEWOOD   DOORS DECORATED IN MARQUETRY.   DESIGNED
AND EXECUTED BY "DIM," PARIS

COUCH   DESIGNED   BY   LOUIS   SOGNOT,   (ATELIER   PRIMAVERA)   PRODUCED   BY   MAGASINS   DU
PRINTEMPS, PARIS

TWO MIRRORS IN CARVED AND GILDED FRAMES DESIGNED BY D. PECHE, VIENNA, EXECUTED BY THE
WIENER WERKSTÄTTE, VIENNA

SIDEBOARD DESIGNED AND EXECUTED BY J. AND M. LELEU, PARIS

SIDEBOARD AND CUPBOARD IN INLAID
TROPICAL WOODS, DESIGNED AND
EXECUTED BY "HAUS UND GARTEN,"
VIENNA

LACQUERED SCREEN—"THE DUCKS"
—DESIGNED BY JEAN DUNAND,
ARCHITECT, 72, RUE HALLÉ, PARIS

SIDEBOARD IN WALNUT, WITH EBONY CUT EDGES, DESIGNED BY
P. WAALS, CHALFORD, GLOS.

TALLBOY IN WALNUT, WITH BRONZED FAN-SHAPED HANDLES, AND BUREAU IN WALNUT AND LIANO,
VENEERED ON MAHOGANY. DESIGNED BY J. DUGALD STARK: EXECUTED BY PETER JONES LTD.,
THE STARK DEPARTMENT, SLOANE SQUARE, LONDON.

DRESSING TABLE AND BEDSTEAD IN MAHOGANY AND EBONY, DESIGNED BY PAUL BROMBERG.
EXECUTED BY H. PANDER EN ZONEN, THE HAGUE, HOLLAND

TABLE IN OAK, DESIGNED BY PAUL BROMBERG, EXECUTED BY H. PANDER EN
ZONEN, THE HAGUE

WRITING TABLE IN OAK, DESIGNED BY PAUL BROMBERG, EXECUTED BY H. PANDER EN ZONEN.
THE HAGUE

SILVER CABINET AND SIDEBOARD IN MACASSAR EBONY: COLOURED MARQUETRY
MOTIFS AND BANDS: SILVERED TASSEL HANDLES ON A BLUE BACK-PLATE.
DESIGNED BY FRED COHEN: EXECUTED BY B. COHEN AND SONS, LTD.,
1-19, CURTAIN ROAD, LONDON

BUREAU IN PALISANDER DESIGNED BY JEAN AND JACQUES ADNET, PARIS

CUPBOARD IN VARNISHED PALISANDER DESIGNED BY JEAN AND JACQUES ADNET: PRODUCED
BY OLIVIER-DESBORDES, PARIS

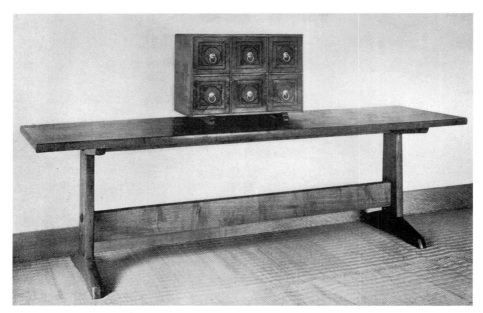

HALL OR SIDE-TABLE IN OAK, WITH OAK NEST OF SIX DRAWERS, DESIGNED BY P. WAALS, CHALFORD, GLOS.

DINING ROOM CHAIR IN WALNUT, WITH HOLLOW WOOD BACK AND UPHOLSTERED SEAT, INLAID WITH EBONY AND SYCAMORE. DESIGNED BY C. A. RICHTER: EXECUTED BY THE BATH CABINET MAKERS' COMPANY, LTD., LOWER BRISTOL ROAD, BATH.

ARMCHAIR IN WALNUT DESIGNED BY GORDON RUSSELL: EXECUTED BY THE RUSSELL WORKSHOPS, LTD., BROADWAY, WORCS.

FURNITURE DESIGNED BY GORDON RUSSELL : EXECUTED BY THE RUSSELL WORKSHOPS, LIMITED, BROADWAY, WORCS.

(Left) Walnut Cabinet for a hall, with drawers and cupboard. (Right) Dressing-table in oak, with walnut candlesticks in turned oak, and fall front writing-table in walnut, with ebony handles and inlay

WORK-TABLE OF SPANISH MAHOGANY,
INLAID, DESIGNED BY A. ROMNEY GREEN,
CHRISTCHURCH

WARDROBE IN ENGLISH OAK, DESIGNED AND EXE-
CUTED BY CROSSLEY AND BROWN, 1035, FINCHLEY
ROAD, GOLDER'S GREEN

TALLBOY IN PLAIN WAXED OAK, DESIGNED
BY LAURENCE A. J. ROWLEY: EXECUTED
BY THE ROWLEY GALLERY OF DECORA-
TIVE ART, 140-2, CHURCH STREET,
LONDON, W. 8

LACE OR GLOVE BOX OF WALNUT, INLAID WITH
BOXWOOD, LABURNUM, CHERRY AND YEWTREE.
DESIGNED BY GORDON RUSSELL: EXECUTED BY THE
RUSSELL WORKSHOPS LTD., BROADWAY, WORCS.

HAND EMBOSSED SCREEN OF
SHEEP SKIN DESIGNED BY
D. PECHE: EXECUTED BY
WIENER WERKSTÄTTE, VIENNA

RED LACQUERED SIDEBOARD DESIGNED BY JOSEF
HOFFMANN: CHINA DESIGNED AND EXECUTED BY
WIENER WERKSTÄTTE, VIENNA

SIDEBOARD IN GERMAN WALNUT DESIGNED BY JOSEF HOFFMANN: EXECUTED BY
ANTON POSPISCHIL, VIENNA

WHITE LACQUERED DINING
ROOM FURNITURE DESIGNED BY
JOSEF HOFFMANN: EXECUTED
BY WENZEL HOHLMANN, VIENNA

BUREAU IN SHARK-SKIN, IVORY AND SNAKE-SKIN, INTERIOR
VARNISHED CORAL COLOUR, DESIGNED BY RENÉ JOUBERT AND
PH. PETIT: PRODUCED BY "DIM," PARIS

LOBBY WRITING-TABLE FOR A NEW YORK APARTMENT HOUSE. DESIGNED BY JONES AND
ERWIN: MIRROR BY FERROBRANDT: ARCHITECTS, HENRY S. CHURCHILL AND HERBERT
LIPPMAN

CABINET DESIGNED BY JEAN BÉTAILLE:
PRODUCED BY SADDIER ET SES FILS, PARIS

DRESSING-TABLE IN EBONY; MIRROR AND
ELECTRIC LIGHT FITTINGS IN SILVERED
STEEL: DESIGNED BY PIERRE CHAREAU.
BRUSHES, ETC., BY PUIFORCAT, PARIS

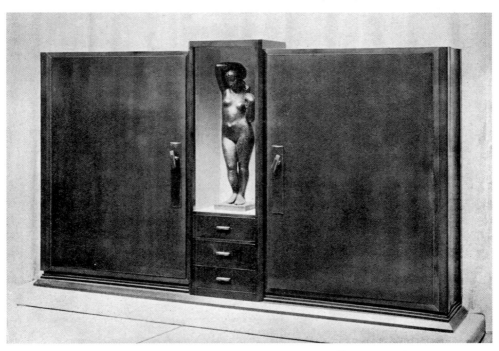

LACQUERED CABINET FOR A COLLECTOR, DESIGNED BY "DOMINIQUE," PARIS

(*above*) *KEM WEBER, 7046, Hollywood Boulevard, Hollywood, U.S.A.   Twin beds and night stand in silvered wood with black rubbed lacquer.   Executed by Barker Bros., Inc., Los Angeles.   (below) PAUL T. FRANKL.   Skyscraper bookcase with lacquer finish, console table, wing chairs upholstered in red English morocco, aeroplane chair on left.   Low mirror-top coffee table in rosewood and ebony.   Wall hung with Japanese wood veneer paper.   Executed by Frankl Galleries, 4, East 48th Street, New York.*

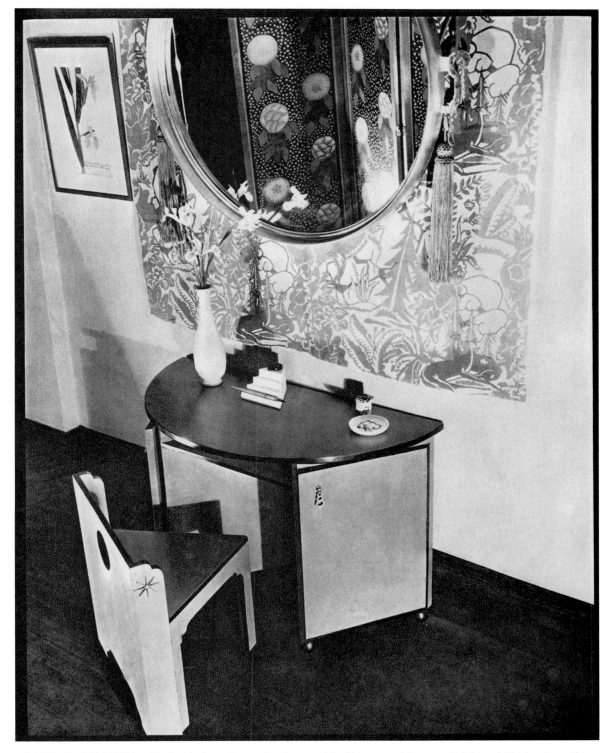

PAUL T. FRANKL. Desk, chair and round mirror, with Chinese red lacquer finish and black trim. The desk handles are silver-plated. Executed by Frankl Galleries, 4, East 48th Street, New York.

J. J. ADNET, Paris. Bedroom suite in palissander and white maple, produced by the Compagnie des Arts Français. Walls distempered blue.

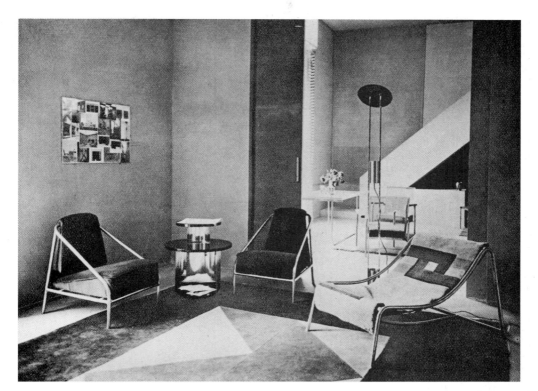

(above) RENÉ HERBST (designer and producer), Paris. Nickelled "tube" furniture with leather cushions. (below) A. FRÈCHET, Paris. Dining room furniture in satin-wood, marquetry panel and silvered bronze figures. Produced by E. VÉROT, Paris

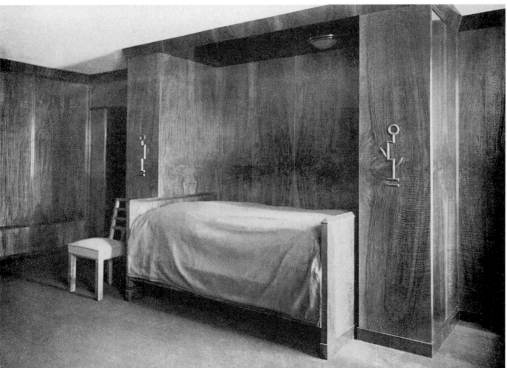

*(Above) Sideboard in rose-wood.   Designed by TOMASO BUZZI, Milan ; executed by Labirinto.   (Below)
Bedroom panelled in laminated walnut, with built-in cupboards.   Designed by JOSEF HOFFMANN, Vienna ;
executed by J. Jonasch.*

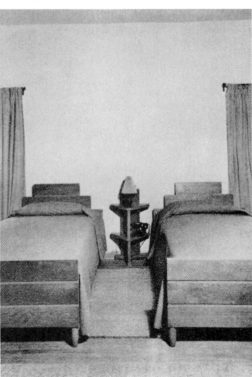

KEM WEBER, 7046, Hollywood Boulevard, Hollywood, U.S.A.   (above) Dresser in grey sage-green lacquered wood.   Full-length mirror, cabinet and seat in silvered wood and black rubbed lacquer. (below, right) Twin beds and night-stand in Oregon pine, stained grey-brown with blue lacquer trim. All executed by Barker Bros., Inc., Los Angeles.   (below, left) PAUL T. FRANKL.   Skyscraper bookcase in contrasting shades of lacquer.   Executed by Frankl Galleries, 4, East 48th Street, New York.

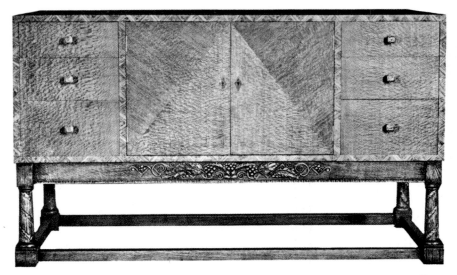

Sideboard in Tasmanian oak banded with elm, and with carved silvered handles and decorations. Produced by B. COHEN & SONS, LTD., Curtain Road, London, E.C.2.

(Left) Wardrobe in unpolished walnut, inlaid with natural coloured woods. (Right) Wardrobe in Bubinga wood, inlaid with black and white lines, and with ivory handles. Designed by J. HULLY : made by THE BATH CABINET MAKERS' CO., LTD., Lower Bristol Road, Bath.

(Above) Fall-front writing cabinet, shown closed and open, in veneered burr elm, inlaid ebony, on walnut base, with ebony inlay and feet: handles and escutcheons in hand-made brass. Designed by GORDON RUSSELL: produced by The Russell Workshops, Broadway, Worcs. (Below) Bedroom suite in French walnut. Designed by J. F. JOHNSON: produced by HEAL & SON, LTD., Tottenham Court Road, London.

(1) *Chest of drawers in weathered oak and zebra wood :* (2) *dressing table in weathered oak and zebra wood :* (3) *bookcase-cupboard in burr walnut, stained and waxed :* (4) *tallboy in cherry wood. Designed by J. DUGALD STARK : produced by PETER JONES, LTD., Sloane Square, London, S.W.3.*

(Above) Dining-room designed to give maximum accommodation in a small flat or house without a proper pantry. Furniture in Coromandel and walnut. Decoration, curtains and upholstery in black and yellow. Table in three pieces, of which centre flap can be used as carving table. (Below) Study, with walls panelled in English walnut veneered on plywood, and furniture in veneered English walnut. Ceiling stippled pale red on gold ground to match red-gold shot curtains. Both rooms designed for WARING & GILLOW, LTD., Oxford Street, London, W.1, by S. CHERMAYEFF.

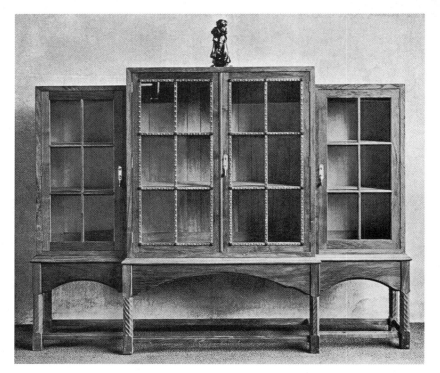

(*Above*) *English walnut bookcase with carved mulberry bars on central doors, silver handles and lock-plates. Designed by GORDON RUSSELL : executed by The Russell Workshops, Ltd., Broadway, Worcs.* (*Below*) *Drawing room at Shortheath Beacon, Farnham, Surrey, panelled in oak veneered on plywood, stained warm grey by " Drytone." Designed by W. J. PALMER JONES, 5 Pembroke Walk Studios, London, W.8.*

(1) and (3) Bog oak chairs, with drop-in seats and ebony splats in back. Designed by GORDON RUSSELL : executed by The Russell Workshops, Ltd., Broadway, Worcs. (2) Man's dressing-chest in grey oak, walnut handles and trim : (7) grey oak dressing-chest and dressing-table, ebony handles and stringing : (8) oak sideboard, laurel wood handles and trim, and oak dining-chair. Designed by MICHAEL DAWN, The Dawn Workshops, Castle Lane, Bedford. (4) Sideboard in unpolished oak. Designed by C. A. RICHTER : executed by BATH CABINET MAKERS' CO., LTD., Lower Bristol Road, Bath. (5) Drawing-room fireplace, with mantelpiece of rose Numidian, black Belge and Roman Stone : grate convertible to gas. Designed by C. H. JAMES, F.R.I.B.A., 15, Gower Street, London, W.C.1. (6) Corner cheval dressing-cabinet of laminated plywood, finished with burnished silver. Designed and executed by L. J. A. ROWLEY, The Rowley Gallery, 140, Church Street, London, W.8.

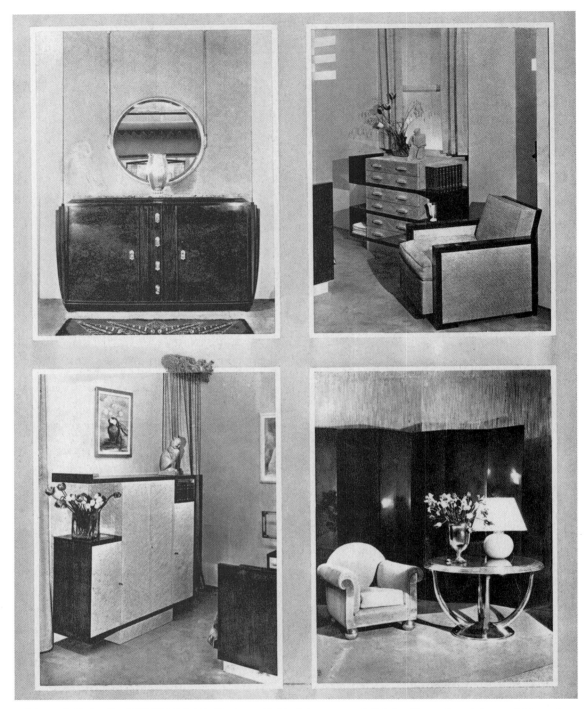

(above, left) P. P. MONTAGNAC, *Paris.   Cabinet in rosewood (photo. Bonney).   (above, right, and below, left)* J. J. ADNET, *Paris.   Bookcase-cupboard and armchair in rosewood and white maple. Cupboard in rosewood and white maple, with mirrors inside the doors.   All produced by the Compagnie des Arts Français (photos. Salaün).   (below, right)* ANDRÉ GROULT, *Paris.   Screen of Chinese lacquer, table and armchair in aluminium*

LÉON BOUCHET, Paris. (above) Bedroom and bathroom. (below) Bedroom furniture in Caucasian oak, bed recess in synthetic lacquer by Charpentier & Brugier. Produced by G. E. & J. DENNERY. Carpets by DA SILVA BRUHNS (photos. Salaün).

WERKSTÄTTEN DER STADT HALLE, *Germany.* (above) *Sideboard in American pine.*
(below) *Lady's sitting room furniture in Caucasian walnut.*

PROFESSOR THIERSCH, Stuttgart. Guest room, with lacquered furniture, for house designed by Peter Behrens. Textiles by EDITH EBERHARDT and BENITA OSSE.

metalwork | Metallarbeiten | Ferronnerie

SILVER-PLATED COFFEE-POT, DECORATED WITH CHASING
DESIGNED AND EXECUTED BY BERNARD CUZNER

SILVER CUP, RAISED AND HAMMERED AND DECORATED WITH
CHASING.   DESIGNED AND EXECUTED BY BERNARD CUZNER

SILVER TEA-POT, RAISED AND HAMMERED AND DECORATED
WITH REPOUSSÉ WORK.   DESIGNED AND
EXECUTED BY BERNARD CUZNER

SILVER BOWL, RAISED AND HAMMERED AND DECORATED WITH APPLIED
WORK.   DESIGNED AND EXECUTED BY ETHEL CUZNER

SILVER TEAPOT, COFFEE-POTS AND JUG DESIGNED AND EXECUTED
BY A. N. KIRK (L.C.C. CENTRAL SCHOOL OF ARTS AND CRAFTS)

SILVER AND ELECTRO-PLATED TEAPOTS, COFFEE-POT AND JUGS DESIGNED AND EXECUTED BY BERNARD CUZNER

SILVER FINGER-BOWL, COMFITURE JAR AND TABLE-BELL DESIGNED AND EXECUTED BY KAJ BOJESEN

SILVER KETTLE AND STAND DESIGNED AND EXE-
CUTED BY GEORG JENSEN

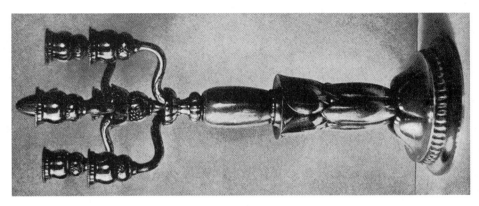

SILVER CANDLESTICK DESIGNED AND EXE-
CUTED BY GEORG JENSEN

SILVER TEA-POT AND STAND DESIGNED AND EXECUTED
BY GEORG JENSEN

SILVER CLOCK, DISH AND COFFEE-POTS DESIGNED AND EXECUTED BY GEORG JENSEN

SILVER COVER DESIGNED AND EXECUTED BY GEORG JENSEN

SILVER CHANDELIER DESIGNED AND EXECUTED BY GEORG JENSEN

SILVER TEA-SET DESIGNED AND EXECUTED BY GEORG JENSEN

SILVER TEA-SET DESIGNED AND EXECUTED BY GEORG JENSEN

SILVER TABLE-WARE DESIGNED AND EXECUTED BY GEORG JENSEN

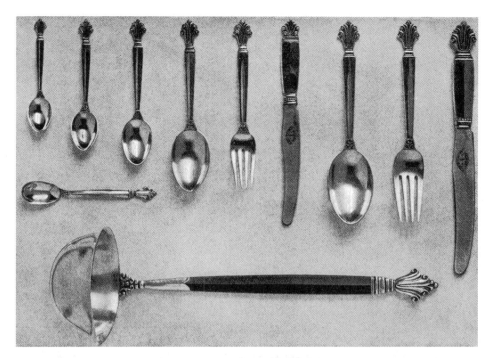

SILVER TABLE-WARE DESIGNED AND EXECUTED BY GEORG JENSEN

SILVER BOWL DESIGNED
BY DR. OSKAR STRNAD,
EXECUTED BY THE
WIENER WERKSTÄTTE

BRASS BASKET AND BOX DESIGNED BY DAGOBERT-PECHE, EXECUTED BY THE WIENER WERKSTÄTTE

SILVER AND IVORY BOXES DESIGNED AND EXECUTED BY RUDOLF JIRASKO (ÖSTERREICHISCHER WERKBUND)

SILVER CIGARETTE CASES DESIGNED BY DAGOBERT-PECHE, EXECUTED BY THE WIENER
WERKSTÄTTE

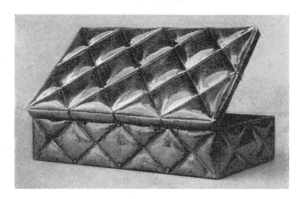

BRASS CIGARETTE BOX
DESIGNED AND EXECUTED
BY KARL HAGENAUER

SILVER BOXES DESIGNED AND EXECUTED BY KARL HAGENAUER

FANLIGHT GRILLE IN WROUGHT IRON DESIGNED AND EXECUTED BY ED. SCHENCK

RADIATOR WITH COPPER GRILLE
DESIGNED AND EXECUTED BY
ED. SCHENCK

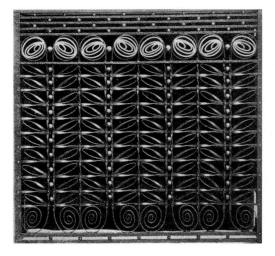

RADIATOR IN WROUGHT IRON WITH
COPPER GRILLE DESIGNED AND EXE-
CUTED BY ED. SCHENCK

WROUGHT-IRON GATES DESIGNED AND EXECUTED BY ED. SCHENCK

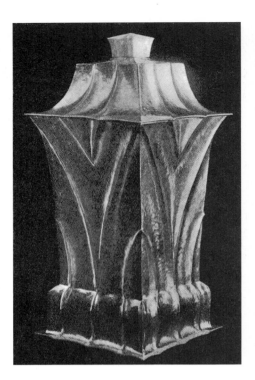

SILVER TEA-CADDY, BOX AND TEA SERVICE DESIGNED BY DAGOBERT-PECHE, EXECUTED BY THE WIENER WERKSTÄTTE

FLOWER-VASE IN HAND-CHASED SILVER, WITH CAST
SILVER HANDLES. DESIGNED AND EXECUTED BY DAVID
ANDERSEN, CHRISTIANIA

SAMOVAR IN HAND-BEATEN SILVER. DESIGNED BY PROF.
DR. JOSEF HOFFMANN, EXECUTED BY THE WIENER WERK-
STÄTTE

SILVER TEA-CADDIE AND TOBACCO BOX, WITH CAST FIGURE AND HAND-CHASED ORNAMENTATION
DESIGNED AND EXECUTED BY DAVID ANDERSEN, CHRISTIANIA

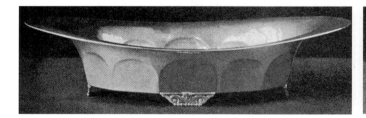

I AND II FILIGREE POWDER-BOXES DESIGNED AND EXECUTED BY G. A. SCHIED, VIENNA; III VASE IN HAND-BEATEN SILVER DESIGNED BY DAGOBERT PECHE, EXECUTED BY THE WIENER WERKSTÄTTE; IV SILVER TEA-SERVICE DESIGNED BY PROF. OTTO PRUTSCHER, EXECUTED BY T. C. KLINKUSCH, VIENNA; V AND VI SILVER CAKE-BASKET AND FLOWER BOWL DESIGNED AND EXECUTED BY DAVID ANDERSEN, CHRISTIANIA

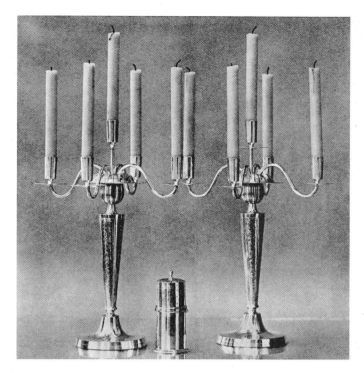

BRASS CANDELABRA DESIGNED AND EXECUTED BY ALOIS WÖRLE, MUNICH

COFFEE MACHINE IN BRASS PLATED WITH GERMAN SILVER WITH ETCHED ORNAMENTATION, HIGHLY POLISHED, DESIGNED AND EXECUTED BY ALOIS WÖRLE, MUNICH. PRESIDENT'S BELL IN BRONZE DESIGNED AND EXECUTED BY P. F. BERNHARD REIMANN, BERLIN

SILVER TEAPOT WITH HANDLE OF LAPIS LAZULI AND SILVER BISCUIT BOX ENRICHED WITH LAPIS LAZULI
DESIGNED AND EXECUTED BY J. PUIFORCAT, PARIS

TEA-SET IN BLACK METAL INCRUSTED WITH SILVER DESIGNED BY JEAN DUNAND, PARIS

COFFEE SERVICE IN SILVER-PLATED BEATEN COPPER DESIGNED AND EXECUTED BY EUGÈNE ET GEORGES CAPON,
PARIS

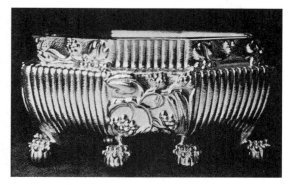

CUT GLASS VASE DESIGNED BY PROF. J. HOFFMANN AND JARDINIERE IN BEATEN SILVER DESIGNED BY D. PECHE EXECUTED BY THE WIENER WERKSTÄTTE

EMBOSSED SILVER, WITH ENGRAVED ACANTHUS LEAVES AND HANDLES OF RUSSIAN LEATHER, DESIGNED AND EXECUTED BY EMIL LETTRÉ, BERLIN

TEA SERVICE IN SILVER AND IVORY DESIGNED BY PROF. J. HOFFMANN AND EXECUTED BY THE WIENER WERKSTÄTTE

SILVER TEAPOT, SUGAR BASIN, MILK JUG, AND HOT WATER JUG. DESIGNED AND EXECUTED BY SÜE ET MARE
(COMPAGNIE DES ARTS FRANÇAIS), PARIS

BRONZE BATH TAPS. DESIGNED AND EXECUTED BY SÜE ET MARE
(COMPAGNIE DES ARTS FRANÇAIS), PARIS

I PEWTER BOWL DESIGNED AND EXECUTED BY JUST ANDERSEN, COPENHAGEN, DENMARK ;
II AND IV SILVER WARE FROM FINLAND ; III SPIRIT KETTLE DESIGNED AND EXECUTED BY
GEORG JENSEN, 56, MADDOX STREET, LONDON ; V ROUND SILVER BASKET ON GLASS AND SILVER
TRAY, AND TWO SILVER BOWLS DESIGNED AND EXECUTED BY JEAN PUIFORCAT, PARIS

BRASS CANDLESTICKS, BOWL, AND DETAIL OF BOWL LID (ABOVE), THE LATTER DESIGNED BY STANLEY PARKER. EXECUTED BY J. P. STEELE, WELWYN GARDEN CITY, HERTFORDSHIRE

HOT WATER JUG, MILK JUG AND COFFEE POT IN PEWTER, WITH STAG-HORN HANDLES DESIGNED AND EXECUTED BY JOHN H. GREEN, DEBDEN, NEAR SAFFRON WALDEN

CANDLESCONCE IN POLISHED WROUGHT IRON WITH PIERCED
PLATE OF GILDING METAL. DESIGNED BY S. GORDON
RUSSELL, AND EXECUTED BY RUSSELL AND SONS, BROAD-
WAY, WORCESTERSHIRE

BOWL IN OXYDISED COPPER WITH PEWTER
APPLIQUÉ DECORATION. DESIGNED AND EXE-
CUTED BY HUGH WALLIS, ALTRINCHAM

WROUGHT COPPER READING LAMP WITH SHADE OF
OYSTERSHELL. DESIGNED BY S. GORDON RUSSELL,
AND EXECUTED BY RUSSELL AND SONS, BROADWAY,
WORCESTERSHIRE

FIRESCREEN IN WROUGHT IRON, "THE NEST,"
DESIGNED AND EXECUTED BY EDGAR BRANDT,
PARIS

FIRESCREEN IN WROUGHT IRON, WITH BRONZE
CIRCLE MOTIF, "DIANA AND GREYHOUND,"
DESIGNED AND EXECUTED BY EDGAR BRANDT

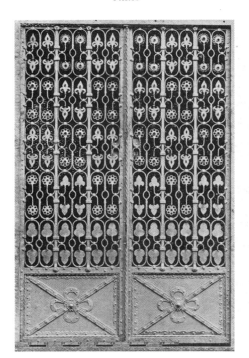

TRELLIS DOOR IN WROUGHT IRON DESIGNED
BY PROFESSOR BLUNCK, AND EXECUTED BY
JULIUS SCHRAMM, BERLIN

PORTAL WITH FORGED FILLINGS DESIGNED BY
PROFESSORS MEBES AND EMMERICH, AND EXECUTED
BY JULIUS SCHRAMM, BERLIN

WROUGHT IRONWORK. DESIGNED
AND EXECUTED BY EDGAR BRANDT,
PARIS

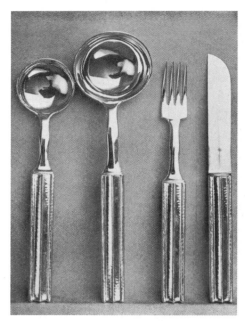

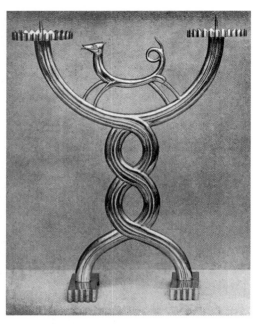

SPOONS, FORK AND KNIFE IN HAMMERED
SILVER DESIGNED BY PROFESSOR JOSEF
HOFFMANN, AND EXECUTED BY THE WIENER
WERKSTÄTTE, G.M.B.H., VIENNA

CANDLESTICK DESIGNED AND EXECUTED BY KARL
HAGENAUER, VIENNA

TEA SERVICE IN SILVER AND BOX-WOOD. DESIGNED BY CHR. FJERDINGSTADT, AND PRODUCED BY
CHRISTOFLE ET CIE, PARIS

BOWL IN HAMMERED STEEL DESIGNED AND EXECUTED BY JEAN
SERRIÈRE, AND PRODUCED BY A. A. HÉBRARD ET CIE, PARIS

SILVERWARE DESIGNED AND EXECUTED BY JEAN PUIFORCAT, PARIS

PEWTER AND BRONZE DESIGNED AND EXECUTED BY JUST ANDERSEN,
COPENHAGEN, DENMARK

TEA SERVICE IN SILVER. DESIGNED BY SVEN MARKELIUS, ARCHITECT, STOCKHOLM, AND
EXECUTED BY ATELIER BORGILA, BARON ERIK FLEMING, STOCKHOLM, SWEDEN

FRUIT SPOON

FRUIT BOWL

GOBLET

CANDELABRA

BISCUIT BOX, WITH SWANS ON LID

ENTRÉE DISH

SILVERWARE DESIGNED AND EXECUTED BY GEORG JENSEN, COPENHAGEN, DENMARK,
AND 56, MADDOX STREET, LONDON

WALL BRACKET HALF LANTERN IN WALNUT AND
GILT WITH OLD AMBER GLASS, DESIGNED AND
EXECUTED BY A. VAN DER VELDE

TWO LIGHT WALL SCONCE IN POLISHED STEEL AND
GILDING METAL, DESIGNED BY GORDON RUSSELL,
EXECUTED BY RUSSELL AND SONS

(*Left and Right*) WROUGHT IRON FIRE DOGS. (*Centre*) POLISHED STEEL FIRE DOG—" WILD GERANIUM,"
DESIGNED BY GORDON RUSSELL AND EXECUTED BY RUSSELL AND SONS, BROADWAY, WORCESTERSHIRE

METAL-WORK DESIGNED AND EXECUTED BY HUGH WALLIS, ALTRINCHAM
Pewter teapot, cream jug and basin (hammered from the sheet metal) standing on oxydised copper tray with pewter appliqué border.

METAL-WORK DESIGNED AND EXECUTED BY HUGH WALLIS, ALTRINCHAM
Biscuit barrel, tea caddies and cigarette box in oxydised copper with decorations in pewter appliqué.

TEA SERVICE DESIGNED AND EXECUTED BY JUST ANDERSEN, COPENHAGEN, DENMARK

COFFEE SERVICE DESIGNED BY GEORG JENSEN, EXECUTED BY GEORG JENSEN'S
SÖLVSMEDIE, COPENHAGEN, DENMARK, AND 15ᵇ NEW BOND STREET, LONDON

BRASS TEA-KETTLE AND STAND DESIGNED BY PARZINGER, BRASS BOWL AND
CIGARETTE BOX DESIGNED BY W. VON WERSIN, EXECUTED BY DEUTSCHE
WERKSTÄTTEN, A.G., MUNICH

DOORWAY IN BUILDING DESIGNED BY
L. AZÉMA, M. EDREI AND J. HARDY,
ARCHITECTS, PARIS, EXECUTED IN
WROUGHT IRON BY NICS FRÈRES, PARIS

METAL-WORK BY JEAN DUNAND, PARIS. (*Left*) TWO JARS INCRUSTED WITH SILVER. (*Right*) LACQUERED VASE

PEWTER WARE BY MAURICE DAURAT, PARIS
(Tea service, vegetable dish, bowls and tobacco jar.)

(*above*) KNIFE, FORK AND SPOON
FOR A CHILD. DESIGNED BY JOSEF
HOFFMANN : EXECUTED BY THE
WIENER WERKSTÄTTE, VIENNA.
(*below*) SILVER VASE BY JEAN
PUIFORCAT, PARIS

SILVER COFFEE POT BY EMIL LETTRÉ, BERLIN

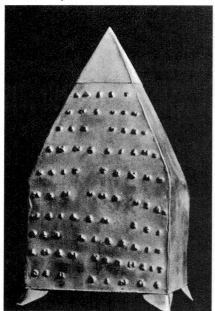

TEA CADDY (FRONT AND REVERSE) IN EMBOSSED SILVER BY LUDWIG GIES, CHARLOTTENBURG,
GERMANY

MIRROR BY RAYMOND SUBES, 131, RUE DAMIEMONT, PARIS

WROUGHT IRON GRILL BY PAUL KISS, PARIS

SILVER COFFEE POT AND JUG, WITH IVORY HANDLES, FROM THE WORKSHOPS OF THE STÄDTISCHE
KUNSTGEWERBESCHULE, HALLE, GERMANY

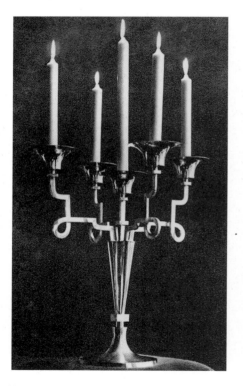

SILVER CANDELABRA BY W. RAEMISCH, STUDENT
AT THE VEREINIGTE STAATSCHULEN, BERLIN—
CHARLOTTENBURG

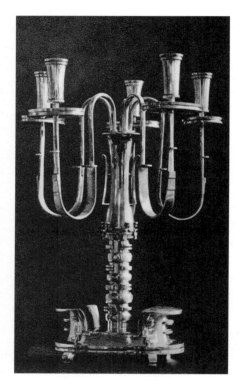

SILVER CANDELABRA BY TH. WENDE, PROFESSOR
AT THE KUNSTGEWERBESCHULE, PFORZHEIM,
GERMANY

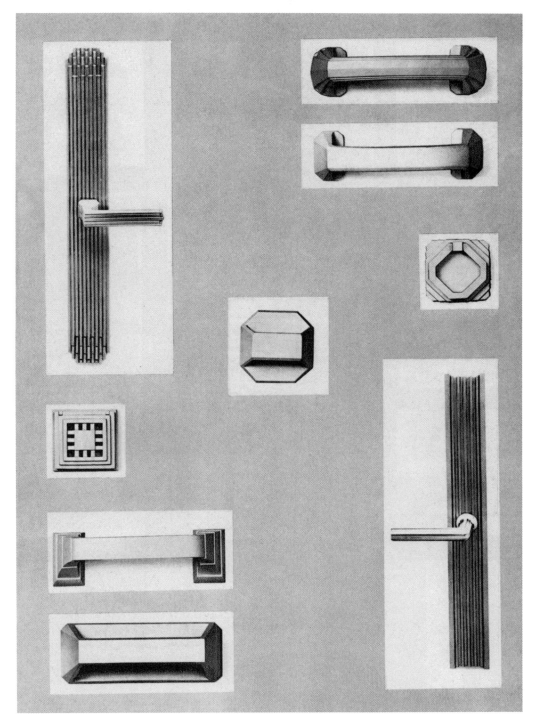

Finger-plates and door handles, designed and executed by L. GIGOU, Paris.

(1)

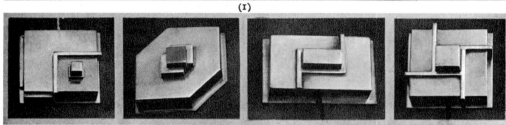

(2)

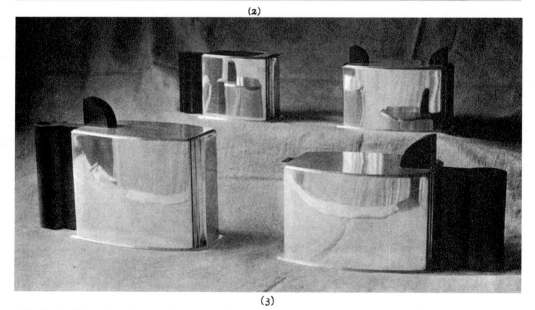

(3)

(1) *Cocktail set in silver, with rosewood and silver tray, designed by VALÉRY BIZOUARD, Paris, produced by TÉTARD FRÈRES.* (2) *Brass table switches, designed and executed by METALLWERKSTAETTEN der SCHULE REIMANN, Berlin.* (3) *Tea service in silver, with ebony handles, designed by JEAN PUIFORCAT, Paris.*

(1) *Fruit bowls in brass, designed by D. PECHE, Vienna: executed by WIENER WERK-STAETTE.* (2) *Powder bowl*, (5) *tobacco jar, designed by JEAN PUIFORCAT and executed in silver for SAKS & COMPANY, Fifth Avenue, New York.* (3) *Silver salver, produced by THE INTERNATIONAL SILVER COMPANY, Meriden, Connecticut (under the direction of Virginia Hamill).* (4) *Pewter bowl on stand, designed by PIERRE DU MONT, Paris (photo. Odiorne).*

ceramics and glass | Keramik und Glas | Céramiques et verrerie

GREEN AND BLACK TEA SERVICE DESIGNED AND EXECUTED BY DOULTON AND CO., BURSLEM

BLUE AND BLACK VEGE-
TABLE DISH DESIGNED
AND EXECUTED BY J.
WEDGWOOD AND SONS,
ETRURIA

UNDERGLAZED BLUE AND GREEN BASIN AND EWER DESIGNED AND EXECUTED BY
J. WEDGWOOD AND SONS, ETRURIA

POTTERY DESIGNED
AND PAINTED BY
ALFRED H. AND
LOUISE POWELL

DESIGNS FOR STAINED GLASS
WINDOWS BY BERNARD RICE

TABLE GLASS EXECUTED BY JAMES POWELL
AND SONS (WHITEFRIARS GLASS WORKS)

PAINTED PLAQUE DESIGNED AND EXECUTED
BY DOULTON AND CO., BURSLEM

STONEWARE BOXES, WITH METAL LIDS, DESIGNED BY P. NORDSTROM
EXECUTED BY THE ROYAL COPENHAGEN PORCELAIN CO.

CRYSTAL GLAZE VASES DESIGNED BY F. LUDVIGSEN, EXECUTED BY THE
ROYAL COPENHAGEN PORCELAIN CO.

STONEWARE VASES DESIGNED BY P. NORDSTROM, EXECUTED BY THE
ROYAL COPENHAGEN PORCELAIN CO.

EARTHENWARE TEA AND DINNER SERVICES DESIGNED BY EDWARD HALD, EXECUTED BY THE RÖRSTRAND WORKS

EARTHENWARE JARS DESIGNED BY WILHELM KAGE, EXECUTED BY THE GUSTAFSBERG WORKS

EARTHENWARE TEA AND DINNER SERVICES DESIGNED BY EDWARD HALD, EXECUTED BY THE RÖRSTRAND WORKS

EARTHENWARE TEA AND DINNER SERVICES, VASES, ETC., DESIGNED BY WILHELM KAGE, EXECUTED BY THE GUSTAFSBERG WORKS

GLASS EXECUTED BY THE ORREFORS WORKS : A, C, D, E, F, G, DESIGNED BY EDWARD HALD ; B, H, BY SIMON GATE

A   B   C

D   F

E

G   H   I

GLASS EXECUTED BY THE ORREFORS WORKS : A, D, E, F, G, I, DESIGNED BY EDWARD HALD ; B, C, H, BY SIMON GATE

POTTERY DESIGNED AND PAINTED BY GABRIEL C. BUNNEY
(L.C.C. CENTRAL SCHOOL OF ARTS AND CRAFTS)

"HAND-CRAFT" POTTERY DESIGNED AND EXECUTED BY CARTER AND COMPANY

POTTERY DESIGNED AND PAINTED BY ALFRED H. AND LOUISE POWELL

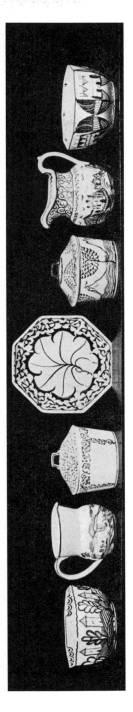

DESIGNED BY OLGA WAGNER

DESIGNED BY HAHN-LOCHER DESIGNED BY OLGA WAGNER DESIGNED BY HEGERMANN-LINDENCRONE

PORCELAIN EXECUTED BY BING AND GRÖNDAHL

PORCELAIN BOX DESIGNED BY
PROF. HANS TEGNER, EXECUTED
BY BING AND GRÖNDAHL

STONEWARE DESIGNED BY C. OLSEN, EXECUTED BY BING AND GRÖNDAHL

STONEWARE DESIGNED BY O. M. LARSEN, EXECUTED BY BING AND GRÖNDAHL

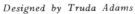

Designed by Truda Adams *Designed by J. Radley Young*

Designed by Truda Adams *Designed by J. Radley Young*

Designed by Harold Stabler *Designed by Truda Adams*

POTTERY EXECUTED BY CARTER, STABLER AND ADAMS

Designed by Truda Adams

Designed by Truda Adams

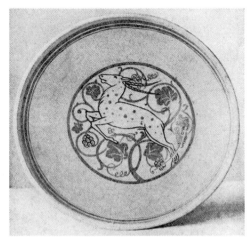

Designed by John Adams

Designed by John Adams
POTTERY EXECUTED BY CARTER, STABLER AND ADAMS

A

B

C

D

POTTERY EXECUTED BY CARTER, STABLER AND ADAMS.   A AND B DESIGNED BY J. RADLEY YOUNG
C AND D DESIGNED BY ERNA MANNERS

POTTERY DESIGNED AND PAINTED BY ALFRED H. AND LOUISE POWELL

CUT-GLASS BOWL DESIGNED BY PROF. JOSEF HOFFMANN

GLASS BOX DESIGNED BY J. ZIMPEL

EXECUTED BY THE WIENER WERKSTÄTTE

POTTERY DESIGNED BY EMMY ZWEYBRÜCK, EXECUTED BY THE VIENNA AND GMUNDEN CERAMIC WORKSHOPS
SCHLEISS, GMUNDEN

POTTERY DESIGNED BY EMMY ZWEYBRÜCK, EXECUTED BY THE VIENNA AND GMUNDEN CERAMIC WORKSHOPS
SCHLEISS, GMUNDEN

POTTERY DESIGNED AND EXECUTED BY THE PAUL REVERE POTTERY, BRIGHTON, MASS.
(DIRECTOR, EDITH BROWN)

POTTERY DESIGNED AND EXECUTED BY THE PAUL REVERE POTTERY, BRIGHTON, MASS.   (DIRECTOR, EDITH BROWN)

CREAM AND BLACK STONEWARE DESIGNED
AND EXECUTED BY BERNARD LEACH, THE
LEACH POTTERY, ST. IVES, CORNWALL

Wedgwood Ware

Millwall Pottery   *Wedgwood Ware*   *Millwall Pottery*

Wedgwood Ware   *Millwall Pottery*   *Wedgwood Ware*

POTTERY DESIGNED AND PAINTED BY ALFRED H. AND LOUISE POWELL, 40, MECKLENBURGH SQUARE, LONDON

Designed by Truda Adams

Designed by John Adams and Ernest Bantten

Designed by Truda Adams

POOLE POTTERY EXECUTED BY CARTER
STABLER AND ADAMS, POOLE, DORSET

POOLE POTTERY BY CARTER, STABLER
AND ADAMS, POOLE, DORSET.—PLATE
DESIGNED BY JOHN ADAMS; POT
DESIGNED BY TRUDA ADAMS

CERAMIC HEAD DESIGNED BY P. VERA, EXECUTED BY MARTIN
COMPAGNIE DES ARTS FRANÇAIS, PARIS

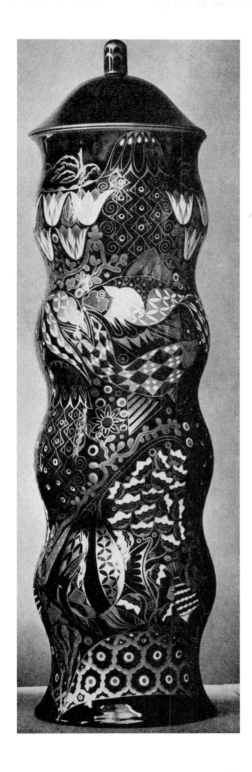

SERAPIS FAIENCE VASE DESIGNED BY KARL KLAUS
VIENNA, EXECUTED BY ERNST WAHLISS, VIENNA

COLOURED CERAMIC FIGURES DESIGNED
AND EXECUTED BY THE WIENER WERK-
STÄTTE

POTTERY DESIGNED BY EUGENE PAULUS, CHATELET

BOWL DESIGNED AND EXECUTED BY THE WIENER
WERKSTÄTTE

JUG AND BOWL DESIGNED AND EXECUTED BY THE WIENER WERKSTÄTTE

MODERN SWISS POTTERY

POTTERY DESIGNED BY PROF. MAX LÄUGER, EXECUTED BY THE GRAND DUCAL MAJOLICA MANU-
FACTORY, KARLSRUHE

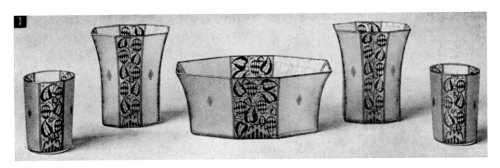

CUT GLASS WITH ENGRAVED ORNAMENTATION
EXECUTED BY J. AND L. LOBMEYR, VIENNA

I DESIGNED BY PROF. JOSEF HOFFMANN; II BY CARL MASSANETZ
III AND IV BY ADOLF ENGEL

CUT GLASS WITH ENGRAVED ORNAMENTATION. DESIGNED
BY PROF. POWOLNY, EXECUTED BY J. AND L. LOBMEYR, VIENNA

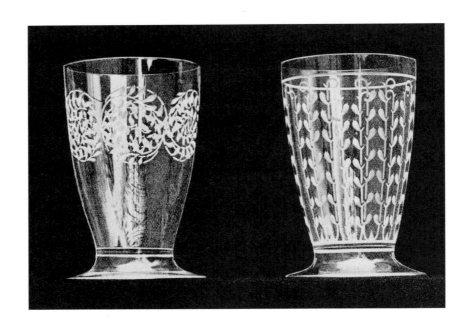

ENGRAVED GLASSWARE DESIGNED BY R. BALLET, PARIS
EXECUTED BY THE COMPAGNIE DES CRISTALLERIES DE BACCARAT

BOWL DESIGNED AND EXECUTED BY R. LALIQUE, PARIS
GLASSWARE DESIGNED BY DAUM FOR THE GLASS MANUFACTORY, NANCY

POTTERY FROM THE WIENER WERKSTÄTTE DESIGNED AND EXECUTED BY D. PECHE, VIENNA

TABLE GLASS MADE BY R. LALIQUE, PARIS

ENAMELLED GLASS BOTTLES WITH SILVER TOPS.   DESIGNED BY ANDRÉ BALLET, VERSAILLES,
PARIS, AND EXECUTED BY LOUIS VUITTON, PARIS

1 AND III STONEWARE MADE BY H. HJORTH, RØNNE ; II STONEWARE MADE BY BING AND GRØNDAHLS, PORCELLÆNSFABRIK, COPENHAGEN, DENMARK

PORCELAIN DESIGNED BY PROF. HANS TEGNER, AND EXECUTED BY BING AND GRØNDAHLS, PORCELLÆNSFABRIK ; AND POTTERY DESIGNED BY KNUD KYHN, AND EXECUTED BY HERMAN A. KÄHLER AND MRS. BLOCK

FRUIT BOWL IN WHITE AND GOLD PORCELAIN ; DINNER SERVICE PLATE IN BLUE AND GOLD
PORCELAIN ; AND DECORATIVE PLATE IN BLUE AND GOLD PORCELAIN. DESIGNED BY
GEO. PONTI, AND EXECUTED BY RICHARD GINORI, DOCCIA, ITALY

TEA SET IN BUTTERCUP YELLOW. DESIGNED BY EDITH BROWN, AND EXECUTED BY THE
PAUL REVERE POTTERY INC., BRIGHTON, MASSACHUSETTS, U.S.A.

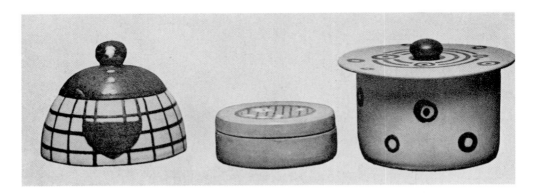

POTTERY MADE BY FRANCIS JOURDAIN, PARIS

STONEWARE DESIGNED BY MME. SOUGEZ, OF THE "ATELIER PRIMAVERA," PARIS

STONEWARE DESIGNED BY MME. CHAUCHET-GUILLERÉ, OF THE "ATELIER PRIMAVERA," PARIS

CANDLESTICKS AND VASES IN MURANO GLASS.   MADE BY CAPPELLIN AND VENINI, VENICE

MURANESE VASES. MADE BY CAPPELLIN AND VENINI, VENICE

MURANO GLASS.   MADE BY CAPPELLIN AND VENINI, VENICE, ITALY :—I AND II CHEESE DISHES, III PRESERVE
DISH, IV PICKLE JAR, V FRUIT DISH

GLASSWARE MADE BY A. DAUM, NANCY, FRANCE

GLASS DESIGNED BY MME. CHAUCHET-GUILLERÉ, OF THE "ATELIER PRIMAVERA," PARIS

TABLE SERVICE IN MURANO GLASS.   MADE BY CAPPELLIN AND VENINI, VENICE

THREE GLASS GOBLETS DESIGNED BY I. HOREJC, AND EXECUTED BY THE ARTEL WORKSHOPS, PRAGUE, CZECHOSLOVAKIA; AND CRYSTAL VASE (GRASSHOPPERS) DESIGNED AND EXECUTED BY R. LALIQUE, PARIS

"NIGHT WATCH," WOLF IN MODELLED GLAZED POTTERY.   DESIGNED AND
EXECUTED BY STELLA R. CROFTS, ILFORD

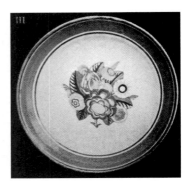

I. AND V.   PAINTED DISHES DESIGNED BY TRUDA ADAMS
II.   POT GLAZED IN EGYPTIAN BLUE BY JOHN ADAMS
III.   PAINTED PLATE DESIGNED BY TRUDA ADAMS
IV. AND VI.   PAINTED POTS DESIGNED BY TRUDA ADAMS

POTTERY EXECUTED BY CARTER, STABLER AND ADAMS, LTD., POOLE, DORSET

HAND-DECORATED POT BY MISS D. BILLINGTON
POTTERY FROG BY L. J. PETERS
UPCHURCH BOWL IN WHITE POTTERY BY MRS. SEYMOUR WAKELY
"MOTHER AND CHILD," SCULPTURED POTTERY BY W. NORTON
SALTGLAZE JAR BY DOULTON AND COMPANY, LTD., LAMBETH, LONDON

(*By courtesy of Messrs. Heal & Son, Ltd.*)

GLASS EXECUTED BY MARINOT AND PRODUCED BY A. A. HÉBRARD ET CIE, PARIS

GLASS EXECUTED BY MARINOT AND PRODUCED BY A. A. HÉBRARD ET CIE, PARIS

CUT GLASS EXECUTED BY MARINOT, AND PRODUCED BY A. A. HÉBRARD ET CIE, PARIS

CUT-GLASS VASES AND BOTTLE EXECUTED BY MARINOT, AND PRODUCED BY A. A. HÉBRARD ET CIE, PARIS

GLASS MADE BY RENÉ LALIQUE, PARIS

GLASSWARE DESIGNED BY MME. SOUGEZ, OF THE ATELIER PRIMAVERA, PARIS

GLASSWARE DESIGNED BY ORLA TUNL NIELSEN, AND EXECUTED BY DEN KONGELIGE PORCELAINSFABRIK AND HOLMEGAARDS GLASSWORKS, COPENHAGEN

TABLE GLASS DESIGNED BY ORLA TUNL NIELSEN, AND EXECUTED BY DEN KONGELIGE PORCELAINSFABRIK AND HOLMEGAARDS GLASSWORKS, COPENHAGEN

GLASSWARE DESIGNED AND EXECUTED BY THE COMPAGNIE CRISTALLERIES DE BACCARAT, PARIS

DISHES AND BRIGHTLY COLOURED VASE DESIGNED BY KÖNIG

ASHTRAYS IN TRANSPARENT GREEN WITH WHITE INTERIORS, DESIGNED BY KÖNIG

HAND-PAINTED BISCUIT JARS AND MARMALADE DISH DESIGNED BY KÖNIG.
POTTERY FROM THE GROSSHERZOGLICHE MAJOLIKA MANUFAKTUR, A.G., KARLSRUHE, GERMANY

I.   STONEWARE COVERED POT, SGRAFFITO AND IRON PIGMENT
II. STONEWARE VASE WITH CHÜN GLAZE OVER BROWN SLIP PATTERN
III. SGRAFFITO SLIPWARE JAR, RED BODY, CREAM SLIP
IV. SGRAFFITO STONEWARE BOTTLE, BROWN ON GREY

POTTERY DESIGNED AND EXECUTED BY BERNARD LEACH, THE LEACH POTTERY, ST. IVES, CORNWALL

CRYSTAL PLATE DESIGNED BY SIMON GATE

CRYSTAL GLASS DESIGNED BY EDWARD HALD

"GRAIL GLASS" IN GREYISH GREEN AND
BROWN DESIGNED BY EDWARD HALD

CRYSTAL BOWLS DESIGNED BY SIMON GATE

GLASSWARE FROM THE ORREFORS BRUKS, A.B. ORREFORS, SWEDEN

STAINED GLASS FOR AN ITALIAN HOUSE.
DESIGNED AND EXECUTED BY P. CHIESA AND
CADORIN, MILAN, ITALY

STAINED GLASS DESIGNED AND EXECUTED
BY P. CHIESA, MILAN, ITALY

I. AND II.   PORCELAIN DESIGNED BY JEAN GAUGUIN, AND EXECUTED BY BING
AND GRØNDAHL, COPENHAGEN, DENMARK
III.   PORCELAIN DESIGNED BY WILHELM KÄGE, AND EXECUTED BY GUSTAVSBERGS
PORSLINSFABRIK, GUSTAVSBERG, SWEDEN

"RELIEF" SERVICE.   DESIGNED BY WILHELM KÄGE, AND EXECUTED BY GUSTAVSBERGS PORSLINS-
FABRIK, GUSTAVSBERG, SWEDEN

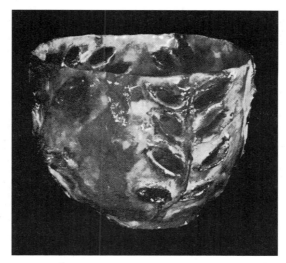

CUP IN FAÏENCE WITH OPEN WORK FLOWER PATTERN.
DESIGNED BY ANTONIE MUTTER, AND EXECUTED BY
STEINGUTFABRIKEN VELTEN-VORDAMM, GERMANY

BISCUIT BOXES DESIGNED BY EMANUEL JOSEF MARGOLD, ARCHITECT, DARMSTADT,
GERMANY

TEA SERVICE DESIGNED BY PROFESSOR OTTO PRUTSCHER, AND EXECUTED BY THE AUGARTEN
PORZELLANFABRIK, VIENNA, AUSTRIA

DINNER SERVICE IN GREY FAÏENCE, DESIGNED AND EXECUTED BY JEAN LUCE, PARIS

VASES IN LONGWY FAÏENCE, WITH RAISED ENAMEL DECORATION BY CLAUDE LÉVY. FROM THE ATELIER PRIMAVERA, PARIS

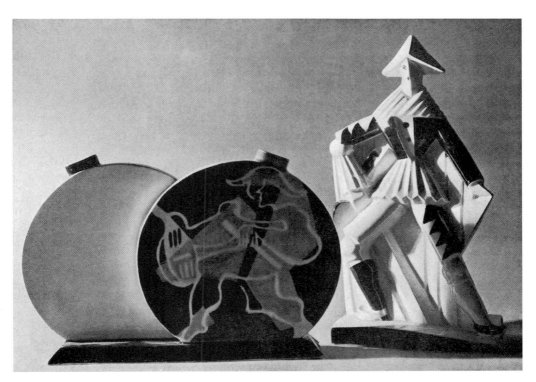

BLACK AND WHITE FAÏENCE; DISCS DESIGNED BY MME. SOUGEZ; STATUETTE DESIGNED BY CLAUDE LÉVY, AND MODELLED BY CHASSAING. FROM THE ATELIER PRIMAVERA, PARIS

DESIGNS FROM THE ROYAL COPENHAGEN PORCELAIN MANUFACTORY (1 and 3)
CELADON PORCELAIN, CRACKLED GLAZE DESIGNED BY TAIS NIELSEN (2)
STONEWARE, DESIGNED BY B. WILLUMSEN

VASE AND INKSTAND DESIGNED BY VALLY WIESELTHIER, EXECUTED BY WIENER
WERKSTÄTTE, VIENNA

POTTERY DESIGNED BY DINA KUHN, EXECUTED BY "BIMINI," VIENNA

POTTERY FROM RICHARD-GINORI MANUFACTURE DI SAN CRISTOFERO, MILAN. *(left and right)* JARS
DESIGNED BY GEO. PONTI, *(centre)* FIGURE DESIGNED BY SAPONAIS

POTTERY DESIGNED BY GEO. PONTI, EXECUTED BY RICHARD-GINORI MANUFACTURE DI SAN
CRISTOFERO, MILAN

MURANESE GLASS, DESIGNED BY
MARTINUZZI, EXECUTED BY VENINI
AND CO., VENICE

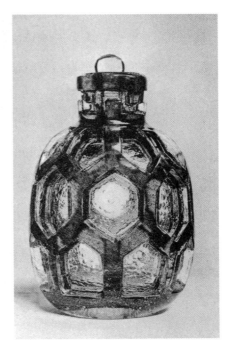

MOULDED AND CUT-GLASS "BIRD" BOTTLE IN
BLUE AND GREEN

MOULDED AND CUT-GLASS BOTTLE IN BLUE
AND GREEN

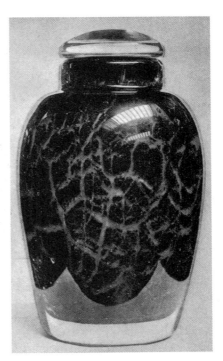

"THE SEA," VERY THICK CRACKLED GLASS

THICK. CRACKLED GLASS

GLASSWARE DESIGNED BY MARINOT; PRODUCED BY GALERIE HEBRARD, 8, RUE ROYALE, PARIS

VASE IN HAMMERED COPPER, SILVER INCRUSTED, DESIGNED AND EXECUTED BY JEAN SERRIÈRE, PRODUCED BY GALERIE HÉBRARD, PARIS

CUT - GLASS BOTTLE DESIGNED AND EXECUTED BY WILHELM VON EIFF, STUTTGART

ENGRAVED GLASSES DESIGNED AND EXECUTED BY THE FACHSCHULE ZWIESEL, BAVARIA

CUT-GLASS BOWL BY ANTON PETER WITT, KARBITZ, DRESDEN

TWO CUT-GLASS VASES BY ANTON PETER WITT, KARBITZ, DRESDEN

CUT-GLASS PLATE, " DILUVIUM," AND CUT-GLASS DISH BY ANTON PETER WITT, KARBITZ, DRESDEN

CUT-GLASS VASE BY ANTON PETER WITT,
KARBITZ, DRESDEN

CUT-GLASS TUMBLER, DESIGNED BY PROF. J.
HOREJC, EXECUTED BY ARTĚL WERKSTATTEN

CRYSTAL VASE. DESIGNED BY O. H.
BRUNNER, PRAGUE, EXECUTED BY
F. MOSER, CARLSBAD

PAINTED JUGS DESIGNED BY TRUDA ADAMS AND MINNIE MCLEISH, EXECUTED BY
CARTER STABLER AND ADAMS, LTD , POOLE, DORSET

TEA-SERVICE DESIGNED BY DORA E. LUNN AND EXECUTED BY THE RAVENSCOURT
POTTERY, RAVENSCOURT PARK, LONDON

TEA-SERVICE DESIGNED BY DORA E. LUNN AND EXECUTED BY THE RAVENSCOURT
POTTERY, RAVENSCOURT PARK, LONDON

ENGLISH SLIP-WARE, REVERTING TO XVIIITH CENTURY WORK, DESIGNED BY MICHAEL CARDEW

STONEWARE BOTTLE, RUST ON BUFF, DESIGNED
BY BERNARD LEACH

STONEWARE BOWL, RUST ON GREY, DESIGNED BY
BERNARD LEACH

FOUR DESIGNS FROM THE LEACH POTTERIES, CORNWALL

FIVE-PIECE TOILET SET IN BROWN SALT-GLAZED STONEWARE. MADE BY JOSEPH
BOURNE AND SON, LTD., DENBY POTTERY, NEAR DERBY

PAINTED CANDLESTICKS. DESIGNED BY JOHN ADAMS. EXECUTED BY CARTER, STABLER
AND ADAMS, LTD., POOLE, DORSET. CANDLES BY PRICE'S PATENT CANDLES, LTD.

TOILET SET. DESIGNED BY JOHN AND TRUDA ADAMS. EXECUTED BY CARTER, STABLER
AND ADAMS, LTD., POOLE, DORSET

VASES BY THE RUSKIN POTTERY, WEST SMETHWICK, BIRMINGHAM: (1) HIGH TEMPERATURE SANG DE BOEUF, WITH IVORY-GREY SHOULDER, (2) IVORY GLAZE WITH BROWN MARKINGS ON CARVED POTTERY STAND; (3) FAWN GLAZE WITH BLUE MARKINGS

POTTERY DESIGNED BY ALFRED H. AND LOUISE POWELL: EXECUTED BY JOSIAH WEDGWOOD AND SONS, STOKE-ON-TRENT

POTTERY BY FRANCES E. RICHARDS, 178, ARCHWAY ROAD, HIGHGATE, LONDON
Honey jar in white and grey opaque glaze : tall pot, thrown, slightly modelled and incised, grey matt glaze and dark mouth : thrown pot, bluish grey glaze, some faint golden-brown, and dark mouth

(1) HAND DECORATED MILK BEAKER AND SAUCER IN MONOCHROME. (2) BREAKFAST CUP AND SAUCER FINISHED IN BUTTERCUP YELLOW, JADE GREEN OR POWDER BLUE. (3) ONE OF A SERIES OF POLITICAL "TOBY" JUGS DESIGNED BY PERCY METCALFE, A.R.C.A., LIMITED TO AN EDITION OF 1,000. EXECUTED BY ASHTEAD POTTERS LTD., VICTORIA WORKS, ASHTEAD. (4) CUP AND SAUCER WITH BLUE AND CORAL DESIGN ON CREAM GROUND. (5) JUG WITH CONVENTIONAL FLORAL DESIGN ON CREAM GROUND, WITH GOLD BAND. EXECUTED BY A. E. GRAY AND CO., LTD., GLEBE WORKS, HANLEY

CABINET OF BLUE AND WHITE KITCHEN JARS DESIGNED BY JOHN ADAMS: EXECUTED BY CARTER, STABLER AND ADAMS, LTD., POOLE, DORSET

POTTERY DESIGNED BY S. OLESIEWITZ (ATELIER PRIMAVERA, PARIS)

STONEWARE POTTERY, DULL BLUE AND RED DESIGN ON A WHITE GROUND, BY CLAUDE
LÉVY (ATELIER PRIMAVERA, PARIS)

POTTERY FROM THE WIENER WERKSTÄTTE, VIENNA. (1) VASE BY GUDRUN BANDISCH. (2) FIGURE
BY SUSI SINGER. (3) VASE BY KITTY RIX

POTTERY DESIGNED BY GIO PONTI : EXECUTED BY RICHARD-GINORI, STABILIMENTE DI DOCCIA, ITALY

VASE OF PRESSED GLASS WITH SILVERED BRONZE
BASE BY P. GENET AND L. MICHON, PARIS

VASE OF ENGRAVED GLASS BY RENÉ LALIQUE, PARIS

TABLE OF ENGRAVED GLASS BY RENÉ LALIQUE, PARIS

From FORTNUM & MASON, LTD., 182, Piccadilly, London, W.1: Large melon-shaped glass vase, with a lovely amethyst grain, about 24 inches high, made in France. Two-handled pot, in a variety of colours, and goblet of canary yellow, 18 inches and 16 inches high respectively, both made in England.

Stoneware by BERNARD LEACH, The Leach Pottery, St. Ives, Cornwall.

(above) *Earthenware by DOROTHIA WARREN-O'HARA, Appletree Lane Pottery, Darien, Conn. :*
(1) shallow bowl, hard fire transparent glaze on underglaze decoration of blue, violet and black : (2) large
bowl, brown-black design on pale green ground, pale buff opalescent glaze : (3) shallow bowl, blue and green
design, transparent glaze : (4) carved bowl, white crackle tin glaze : (5) shallow bowl, engobe of red clay over
buff clay, hard fire transparent glaze : (6) large bowl, engobe of white, lattice divisions of bright green,
transparent crackle glaze. (below) J. HILLERBRAND : china tea set, executed by Deutsche Werkstätten,
Hellerau and Munich.

CORNING GLASS WORKS, 501, *Fifth Avenue, New York City : modern table setting : centre pan and service plates of " Mirror black " glass : footed tumblers of crystal glass, with decorative trim of black glass.*

Murano glassware. (1) *by* VENINI & CO., *Venice :* (2), (3), (4) *and* (5) *by* CAPPELIN & CO., *Venice.*

Porcelain dinner service, designed and produced by ANDREA GALVANI, Pordenone, Italy.
(2), (3), (4) and (5) Plates and coffee set, designed by GIO PONTI, executed by RICHARD-
GINORI, San-Cristofero, Milan.

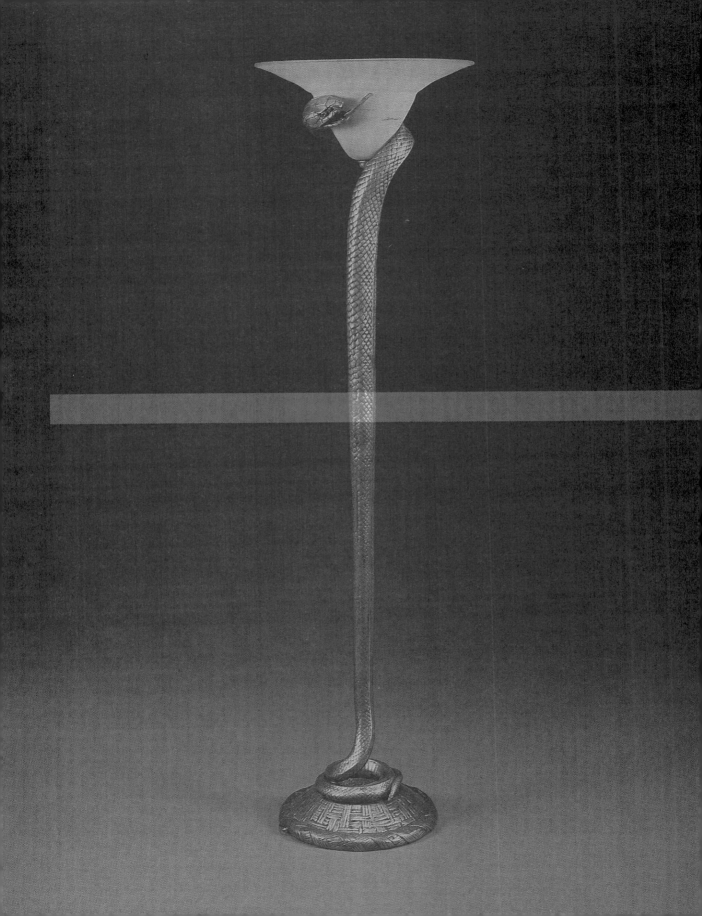

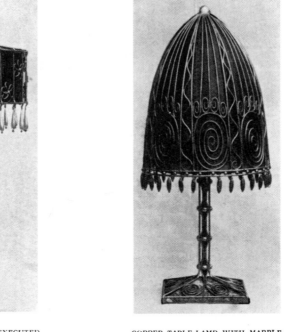

COPPER TABLE-LAMP DESIGNED AND EXECUTED
BY ED. SCHENCK

COPPER TABLE-LAMP WITH MARBLE
BASE DESIGNED AND EXECUTED BY
ED. SCHENCK

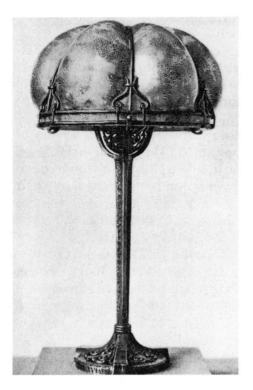

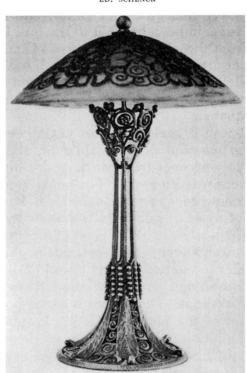

WROUGHT-IRON WORK DESIGNED AND EXECUTED BY EDGAR BRANDT

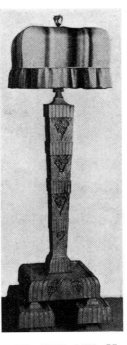

GILDED WOOD LAMP DE-
SIGNED BY DAGOBERT-PECHE,
EXECUTED BY THE WIENER
WERKSTÄTTE

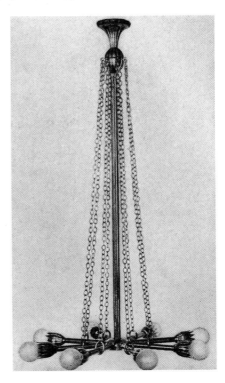

ELECTROLIER DESIGNED BY DAGO-
BERT-PECHE, EXECUTED BY THE
WIENER WERKSTÄTTE

ELECTROLIER DESIGNED BY PROF. JOSEF
HOFFMANN, EXECUTED BY THE WIENER WERK-
STÄTTE

DESIGNED BY PROF. JOSEF HOFFMANN

DESIGNED BY DAGOBERT-PECHE

TABLE-LAMPS EXECUTED BY THE WIENER WERKSTÄTTE

ELECTRIC LIGHT PENDANT IN WROUGHT IRON AND
CRYSTAL GLASS.   DESIGNED BY R. DES DESVALLIERES
COMPAGNIE DES ARTS FRANÇAIS, PARIS

ELECTRIC LIGHT PENDANT IN BLACK AND WHITE GLASS
DESIGNED AND EXECUTED BY ANDRÉ GROULT, PARIS

MARBLE BOWL AND METAL BASKET, WITH ILLUMINATED GLASS FRUIT
DESIGNED BY M. ALEXIS, EXECUTED BY VANDERBORGHT FRÈRES, BRUSSELS

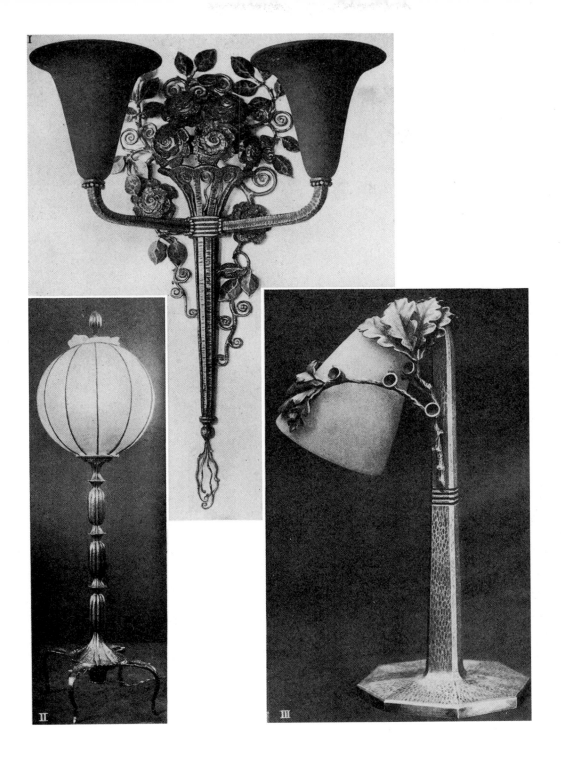

I WROUGHT-IRON ELECTRIC BRACKET DESIGNED AND EXECUTED BY EDGAR BRANDT, PARIS ; II ELECTRIC TABLE-LAMP DESIGNED BY W. FOLLIN, EXECUTED BY THE OESTERREICHISCHER WERKBUND, VIENNA ; III ELECTRIC READING-LAMP IN WROUGHT-IRON   DESIGNED AND EXECUTED BY A. G. SZABO, PARIS

BOWL-FITTING OF SOFT
COLOURED SILK, WITH
NARROW BRAID SILK
CORDS AND TASSELS

BOWL-FITTING OF SOFT
COLOURED SILK, LINED
WHITE, WITH FANCY BRAID
CORDS AND TASSEL

BOWL-FITTING, HAND PAINTED
WITH FANCY BRAID, CORDS
AND TASSELS

STAND IN LUSTRE SATIN, WITH SHADE
IN COLOURED SILK LINED WHITE

STAND IN CORDED VELVET, WITH SHADE
IN SOFT SILK AND STRIPED TAFFETA

ELECTRIC LAMP-SHADES DESIGNED AND EXECUTED BY
W. H. GAZE AND SONS, LTD., KINGSTON-ON-THAMES

I AND III STANDARD ELECTRIC LAMPS, WITH SHADES, DESIGNED AND EXECUTED BY FRANCIS JOURDAIN, PARIS ;
II ELECTRIC LIGHT FITTING, IN GLASS AND IRON WORK, DESIGNED AND EXECUTED BY SÜE ET MARE (COMPAGNIE
DES ARTS FRANÇAIS), PARIS

LAMPS IN GILT BRONZE DESIGNED AND EXECUTED BY THE " ATELIER DE LA MAÎTRISE," PARIS

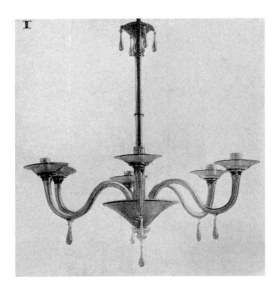

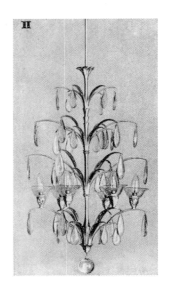

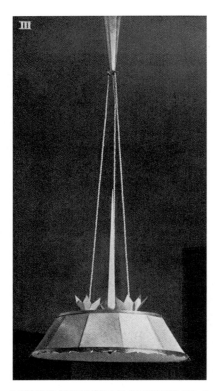

I MURANO LAMP MADE BY CAPPELLIN AND VENINI, VENICE, ITALY ; II AND III ELECTRIC LIGHT
FITTINGS MADE BY MAX KRÜGER, BERLIN, GERMANY ; IV FLORENTINE LAMP IN MURANO GLASS
MADE BY CAPPELLIN AND VENINI

I ELECTRIC LIGHT BRACKET DESIGNED BY HUGO GORGE AND EXECUTED BY R. LORENZ, VIENNA, AUSTRIA ;
II BRONZE HALL LANTERN DESIGNED AND EXECUTED BY H. TVERMOES, COPENHAGEN, DENMARK ;
III ELECTRIC LIGHT BRACKET DESIGNED BY KARL HOFMANN AND FELIX AUGENFELD, AND EXECUTED
BY MELZER AND NEUHARDT, A.G., VIENNA ; IV AND VI CANDLESTICKS IN PEWTER DESIGNED AND
EXECUTED BY JUST ANDERSEN, COPENHAGEN ; V BRASS STANDARD LAMP DESIGNED BY PROFESSOR
OTTO PRUTSCHER, AND EXECUTED BY MELZER AND NEUHARDT, A.G., VIENNA ; VII WOODEN LAMP-
STAND, WITH SILK SHADE, DESIGNED BY I. HAVLÍČEK, AND EXECUTED BY THE ARTĚL WORKSHOPS,
PRAGUE, CZECHOSLOVAKIA ; VIII LAMPSHADE DESIGNED AND EXECUTED IN THE HANS NEUMANN
ARTS AND CRAFTS SCHOOL, VIENNA

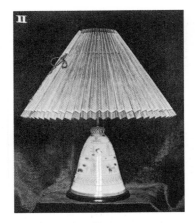

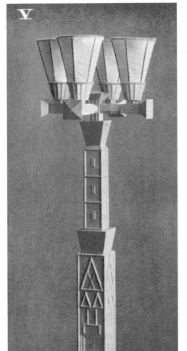

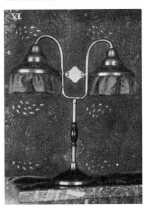

I. AND III. CANDLESTICKS IN HAMMERED SILVER DESIGNED BY PROFESSOR JOSEF HOFFMANN, AND EXECUTED BY THE WIENER WERKSTÄTTE, G.M.B.H., VIENNA, AUSTRIA

II. LAMPSTAND IN FAÏENCE DESIGNED BY CHARLOTTE HARTMANN, AND EXECUTED BY STEINGUT-FABRIKEN VELTEN-VORDAMM, GERMANY

IV. CANDLESTICK EXECUTED BY THE ÉCOLE NATIONALE DES ARTS DÉCORATIFS, POSEN, POLAND

V. AND VIII. STANDARD AND READING LAMPS DESIGNED BY EMANUEL JOSEF MARGOLD, ARCHITECT, DARMSTADT, GERMANY

VI. BRONZE LAMP DESIGNED BY A. J. KROPHOLLER, ARCHITECT, WASSENAAR, HOLLAND

VII. READING LAMP DESIGNED BY FRITZ LEHMANN, ARCHITECT, PRAGUE, CZECHO-SLOVAKIA

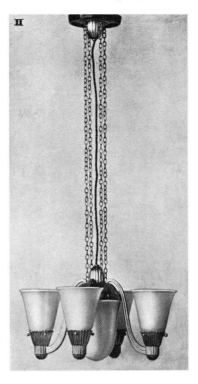

I. AND III. HAMMERED BRASS LAMPS WITH SILK SHADES, AND IV. AND V. HAMMERED SILVER
CANDLESTICKS DESIGNED BY PROFESSOR JOSEF HOFFMANN, AND EXECUTED BY THE WIENER
WERKSTÄTTE, G.M.B.H., VIENNA, AUSTRIA

II., VI. AND VIII. ELECTROLIER AND READING LAMPS DESIGNED BY PROFESSOR OTTO PRUTSCHER,
AND EXECUTED BY THE OESTERREICHISCHER WERKBUND, VIENNA, AUSTRIA

VII. LAMP IN OXYDISED BRONZE DESIGNED BY PROFESSOR DR. JOSEF FRANK, AND EXECUTED BY
THE OESTERREICHISCHER WERKBUND, VIENNA, AUSTRIA

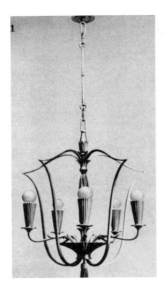

(1) AND (3) BRASS HANGING LAMPS DESIGNED BY PAUL LASZLO, STUTTGART, GERMANY: EXECUTED BY MELZER AND NEUHARDT, VIENNA, (2) WALL SCONCE IN BRASS DESIGNED BY ED. PFEIFFER, KUNSTAKADEMIE, MUNICH, GERMANY

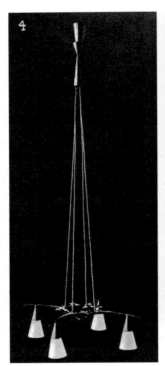

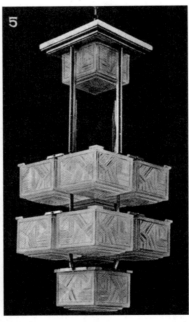

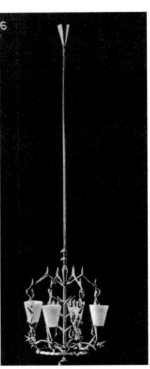

(4) AND (6) HANGING LAMPS BY MAX KRUGER, BERLIN.   (5) HANGING LAMP BY MARIUS SABINO, PARIS

(1)

(2)

(3)

(4)

(5)

(6)

(7)

(8)

(1) and (3) *Wall lamps in moulded, unpolished glass, by P. GENET and L. MICHON, Paris.*
(2) *Crystal chandelier, designed and produced by R. LALIQUE, Paris.* (4) *Candelabra in red enamel with silver edges, designed and made by STÄDT. HANDWERKER & KUNGSTGEWERBE-SCHULE, STETTIN.* (5) *and* (6) *Table lamps of forged iron and opalescent glass, designed by GEORGES CHAMPION: produced by STUDIO GUÉ (Georges and Gaston Guérin).* (7) *Table lamps: on left, with tubular frosted bulbs and nickelled copper: on right, an arrangement of a round frosted bulb and three nickelled copper balls: designed by J. J. ADNET, Paris: produced by Cie. des Arts Français.* (8) *Candelabra in pewter, designed by PIERRE DU MONT, Paris.*

(1) *and* (3) *Water filled glass bowls for electric light, with pleated linen shades. Produced by JAMES POWELL & SONS (WHITEFRIARS), LTD., 98, Wigmore Street, London, W.1. (2) Crystal chandelier, designed by SABINO, Paris. (4) and (6) Table lamps in enamelled metal and brass respectively, with parchment shades. Designed and made by STÄDT. HANDWERKER & KUNST-GEWERBESCHULE, STETTIN, Germany. (5) Table lamp in fawn and jade green glaze, designed and made by THE RUSKIN POTTERY (W. Howson Taylor), West Smethwick. (7) Table lamp in Murano glass, by CAPPELIN & CO., Venice. (8) Bedside lamp in carved ivory, designed by EVE LE BOURGEOIS, Paris. (9) Ceramic table lamp, designed by VALLY WIESELTHIER, Vienna : executed by WIENER WERSTAETTE.*

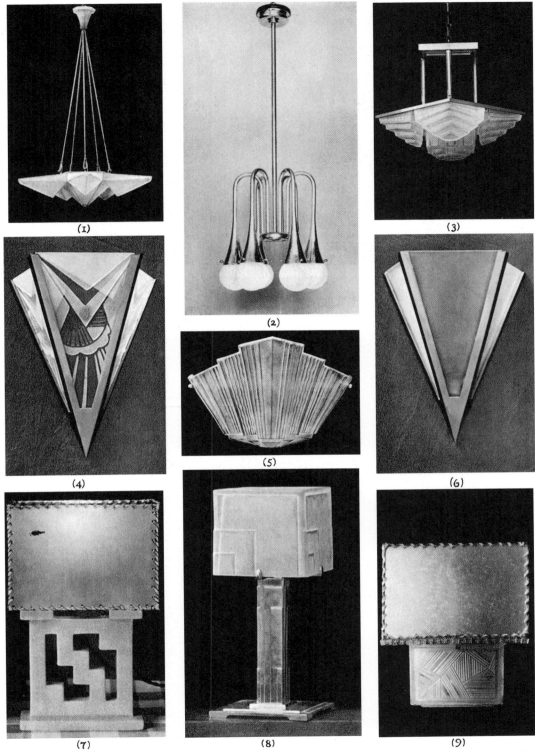

(1), (5) and (8) *Chandelier, table lamp and wall lamp in moulded, unpolished glass, by P. GENET and L. MICHON, Paris.* (2) *Brass electrolier, designed by JOSEF HOFFMANN, Vienna: executed by WIENER WERKSTAETTE.* (3) and (9) *Crystal chandelier and table lamp, by SABINO, Paris.* (4) and (6) *Wall lamps in silvered metal and engraved and enamelled glass, designed by P. POUCHOL, produced by LA MAÎTRISE, Paris (Galeries Lafayette).* (7) *Table lamp in fretted faïence, by ROBERT LALLEMANT, Paris.*

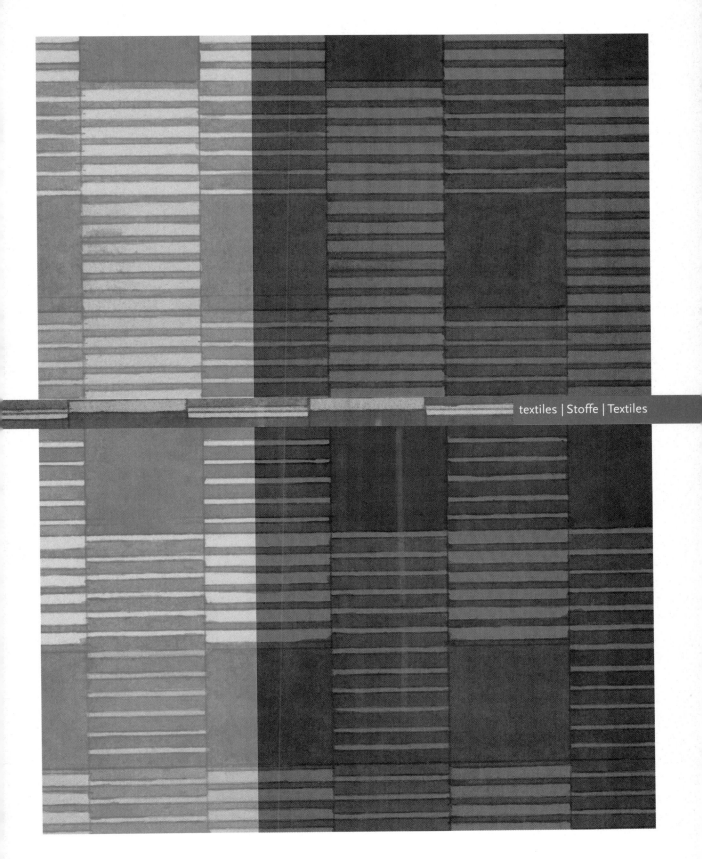

textiles | Stoffe | Textiles

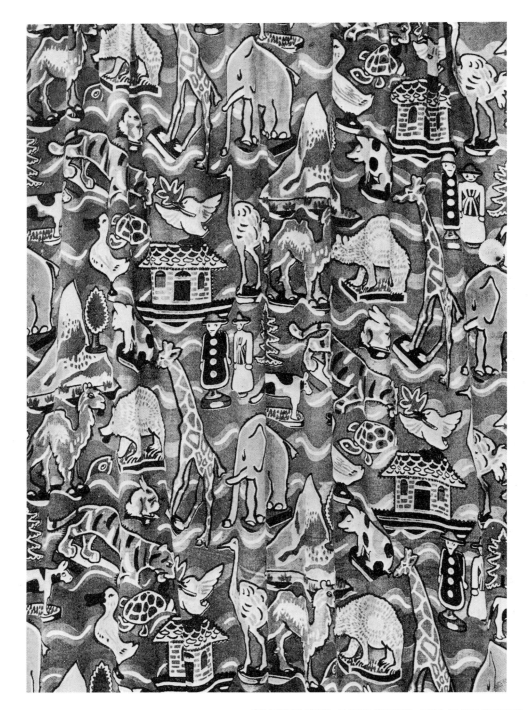

CRETONNE DESIGNED BY DOROTHY
HUTTON, EXECUTED BY W. FOXTON

DESIGN FOR CRETONNE
BY E. HOPPÉ

CRETONNE DESIGNED BY W. TURNER
EXECUTED BY W. FOXTON

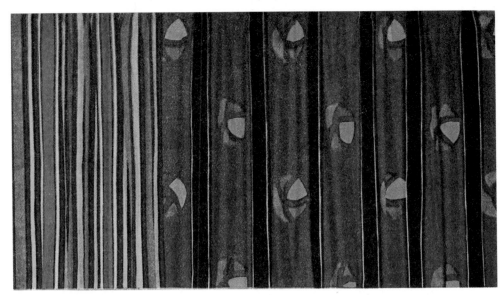

WOVEN FABRIC
DESIGNED BY MINNIE McLEISH

PRINTED FABRIC DESIGNED BY C. LOVAT FRASER

CRETONNE
DESIGNED BY GLADYS BARRACLOUGH

WOVEN FABRIC DESIGNED BY W. FOXTON

TEXTILE FABRICS EXECUTED BY W. FOXTON

DETAIL OF EMBROIDERED CURTAIN
BY E. RUTH RAYNER

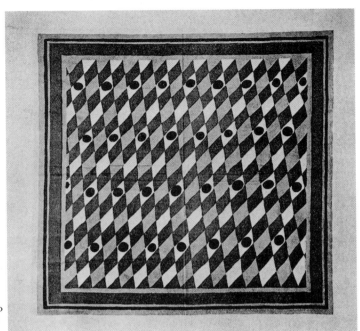

COTTON TABLE-COVER DESIGNED
BY MINNIE MCLEISH FOR W.
FOXTON

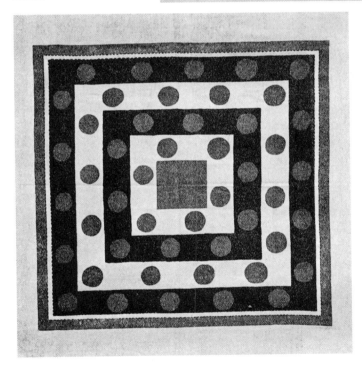

COTTON TABLE-COVER DESIGNED
BY MINNIE MCLEISH FOR W.
FOXTON

MACHINE-PRINTED CRETONNE DESIGNED BY MINNIE McLEISH FOR W. FOXTON

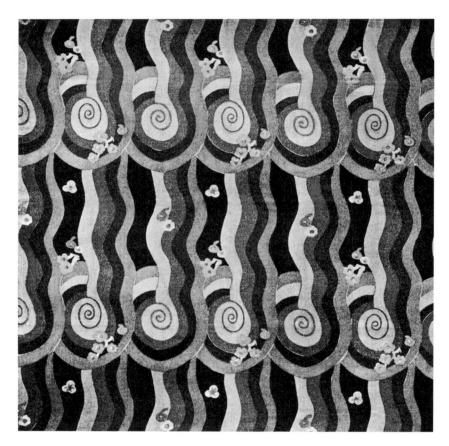

MACHINE-PRINTED CRETONNE DESIGNED BY GLADYS BARRACLOUGH FOR W. FOXTON

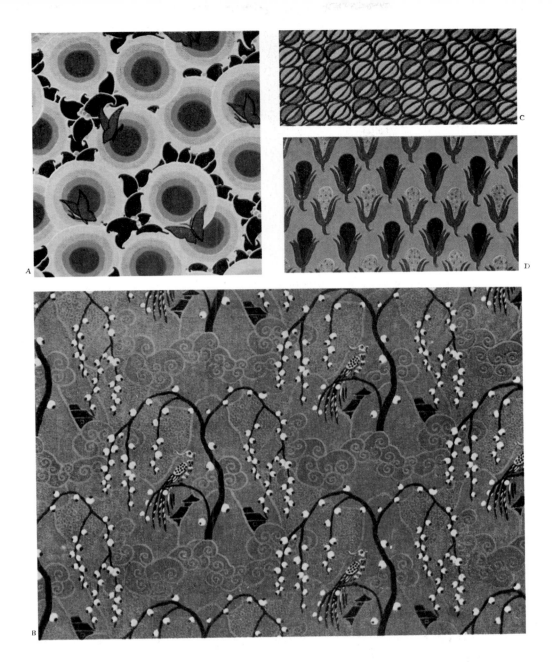

A AND B—LINEN AND COTTON BLOCK PRINTS BY W.
FOXTON: C AND D—MACHINE PRINTED CRETONNES
DESIGNED BY MINNIE McLEISH FOR W. FOXTON

BATIK HANGING
BY E. O. HOPPE

DESIGN FOR CRETONNE BY F. GREGORY BROWN.

BATIK DESIGN BY
COR DE WOLFF

BATIK DESIGN BY COR DE WOLFF

"QUEEN GUINEVER GOES A-MAYING." BATIK OVERMANTEL BY JESSIE M. KING

DESIGN FOR EMBROIDERED BED-HANGING BY FLORENCE DUNNETT
(EDINBURGH COLLEGE OF ART, DEPARTMENT OF APPLIED ART)

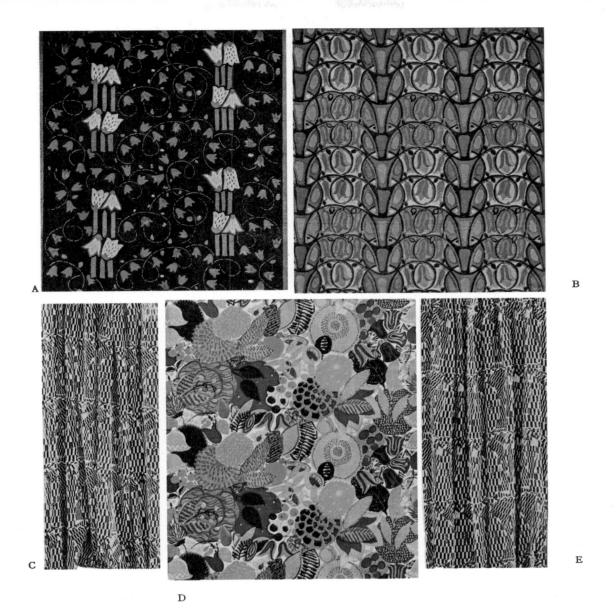

A—CRETONNE DESIGNED BY CONSTANCE IRVING;
B AND D—CRETONNES DESIGNED BY MINNIE
McLEISH; C AND E—VOILE DESIGNED BY C. R.
MACINTOSH. ALL PRODUCED BY W. FOXTON

TABLE-MATS OF DARNED NET DESIGNED BY EMMY ZWEYBRÜCK, EXECUTED IN THE ZWEYBRÜCK WERKSTÄTTE

TABLE-MAT OF DARNED NET DESIGNED BY EMMY ZWEYBRÜCK, EXECUTED IN THE
ZWEYBRÜCK WERKSTÄTTE

FOUR EMBROIDERED CUSHIONS DESIGNED BY MÖHL
FROM THE CLARA WÄVER ESTABLISHMENT

WALL-HANGING DE-
SIGNED BY MÖHL
FROM THE CLARA
WÄVER ESTABLISH-
MENT

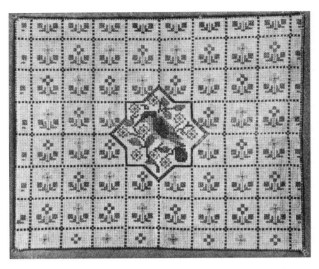

EMBROIDERED PANEL IN CROSS-STITCH BY WINIFRED LAW
(SCHOOL OF ART, WALSALL)

EMBROIDERED BAG IN CROSS-STITCH
BY NORAH BOWEN (SCHOOL OF ART,
WALSALL)

EMBROIDERED BAG BY LUCY SAMP-
SON (EDINBURGH COLLEGE OF
ART, DEPARTMENT OF APPLIED ART)

EMBROIDERED BORDER IN CROSS-STITCH BY M. FRANKHAM
(SCHOOL OF ART, WALSALL)

EMBROIDERED MOUNTED
COVERLET BY ROSA LEO

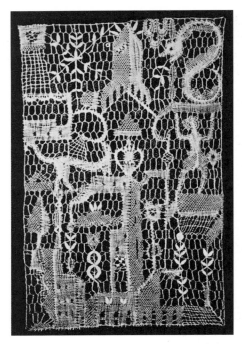

PILLOW LACE FROM THE WIENER WERKSTÄTTE
DESIGNED BY ANNY EHRENFELD SCHRÖDER

LINEN FABRIC DESIGNED BY P. DARIEL, PARIS
(*Colours: Black, brown and scarlet on white*)

LINEN FABRICS—" LES COURGES " AND " MONNAIE DU PAPE " DESIGNED BY FRANCIS JOURDAIN, PARIS

A PANEL OF TORFYN TAPESTRY DESIGNED BY JEAN ORAGE AND WOVEN BY " THE SCOTTISH FOLK FABRICS "

TWO WALL-PAPERS PRODUCED BY ARTHUR SANDERSON AND SONS LTD., 52-55, BERNERS STREET, LONDON, (RIGHT) DESIGNED BY LÉON BAKST

DESIGNS FROM "MODERN TEXTILES," 46, BEAUCHAMP PLACE, LONDON. (*Left and right*)
LINENS DESIGNED AND PRINTED BY FRANCES WOOLLARD AND ENID MARX RESPECTIVELY; (*centre*)
BATIK ON LINEN BY MARION DORN; (*in front*) COTTON DESIGNED BY PAUL NASH AND PRINTED
BY "FOOTPRINTS"

(Left) HAND PRINTED SHANTUNG,
" TOADSTOOLS "; (right) PRINTED
CRÊPE DE CHINE, " BATHERS,"
BY PHYLLIS DONALDSON, A.R.C.A.,
59, WARWICK ROAD, LONDON.

Index
Designers, architects and manufacturers
Designer, Architekten und Hersteller
Designers, architectes et fabricants

l. = left / links / à gauche
r. = right / rechts / à droite
t. = top / oben / ci-dessus
c. = centre / Mitte
b. = bottom / unten / ci-dessous

Credits
Bildnachweis
Crédits photographiques

DECORATIVE ART SERIES

Decorative Art – 1900s & 1910s
Ed. Charlotte & Peter Fiell
576 pages
3–8228–6050–6
[ENGLISH/GERMAN/FRENCH]

Decorative Art – 1950s
Ed. Charlotte & Peter Fiell
576 pages
3–8228–6619–9
[ENGLISH/GERMAN/FRENCH]

Decorative Art – 1920s
Ed. Charlotte & Peter Fiell
576 pages
3–8228–6051–4
[ENGLISH/GERMAN/FRENCH]

Decorative Art – 1960s
Ed. Charlotte & Peter Fiell
576 pages
3–8228–6405–6
[ENGLISH/GERMAN/FRENCH]

Decorative Art – 1930s & 1940s
Ed. Charlotte & Peter Fiell
576 pages
3–8228–6052–2
[ENGLISH/GERMAN/FRENCH]

Decorative Art – 1970s
Ed. Charlotte & Peter Fiell
576 pages
3–8228–6406–4
[ENGLISH/GERMAN/FRENCH]